The Middle Passage

Marie-Louise von Franz, Honorary Patron

**Studies in Jungian Psychology
by Jungian Analysts**

Daryl Sharp, General Editor

The Middle Passage
From Misery to Meaning in Midlife

JAMES HOLLIS

For Jill, and for Taryn and Timothy, Jonah and Seah

"And then comes the knowing that in me there is space for a second, large, and timeless life."
("Ich liebe meines Wesens Dunkelstunden.")—Rainer Maria Rilke.)

Canadian Cataloguing in Publication Data

Hollis, James
   The middle passage: from misery to meaning in midlife

(Studies in Jungian psychology by Jungian analysts; 59)

Includes bibliographical references and index.

ISBN 0-919123-60-0

1. Middle age—Psychological aspects.
2. Jung, C.G. (Carl Gustave), 1875-1961.
I. Title. II. Series.

BF724.6.H64 1993   155.6'6   C92-095112-0

INNER CITY BOOKS
Box 1271, Station Q, Toronto, Canada M4T 2P4
Telephone (416) 927-0355
FAX (416) 924-1814

Honorary Patron: Marie-Louise von Franz.
Publisher and General Editor: Daryl Sharp.
Senior Editor: Victoria Cowan.

INNER CITY BOOKS was founded in 1980 to promote the understanding and practical application of the work of C.G. Jung.

Cover: "Pursuing the Eons" (1987), by Jerry Pethick; etched mirror, glass, aluminum, silicon spectrafoil, payne skin, enameled steel and copper. Photo by Bob Cain. (Publisher's collection)

Index by Daryl Sharp

Printed and bound in Canada by
University of Toronto Press Incorporated

CONTENTS

See last page for descriptions of other Inner City Books

Mid-way in life's journey
I found myself in a dark wood,
having lost the way.
—Dante, *The Inferno.*

Our hearts have overbrimmed new agonies, with new
luster and silence. . . . The mystery has grown
savage, and God has grown greater. The dark
powers ascend, for they have also grown greater,
and the entire human island quakes.
—Nikos Kazantzakis, *The Saviors of God.*

Life must be remembered backward, but lived forward.
—Soren Kierkegaard, *The Journals of Kierkegaard.*

If you bring forth what is within you, what
you bring forth will save you. If you do
not bring forth what is within you,
what you do not bring forth will destroy you.
—*The Gospel According to Thomas.*

Preface

Why do so many go through so much disruption in their middle years? Why then? Why do we consider it to be a crisis? What is the meaning of such an experience?

The midlife crisis, which I prefer to call the Middle Passage, presents us with an opportunity to reexamine our lives and to ask the sometimes frightening, always liberating, question: "Who am I apart from my history and the roles I have played?" When we discover that we have been living what constitutes a false self, that we have been enacting a provisional adulthood, driven by unrealistic expectations, then we open the possibility for the second adulthood, our true personhood.

The Middle Passage is an occasion for redefining and reorienting the personality, a rite of passage between the extended adolescence of first adulthood and our inevitable appointment with old age and mortality. Those who travel the passage consciously render their lives more meaningful. Those who do not, remain prisoners of childhood, however successful they may appear in outer life.

My psychoanalytic practice over the last decade has been predominantly composed of people in the Middle Passage, and I have seen the pattern again and again. The Middle Passage represents a wonderful, though often painful, opportunity to revision our sense of self. Accordingly, this book will address the following issues:

How did we acquire our original sense of self? What are the changes which herald the Middle Passage? How do we redefine our sense of self? What is the relationship between Jung's concept of individuation and our commitment to others? What are the attitudes and behavioral changes which support individuation and move us, via the Middle Passage, from misery to meaning?

Depth psychologists know that the capacity for growth depends on one's ability to internalize and to take personal responsibility. If we forever see our life as a problem caused by others, a problem to be "solved," then no change will occur. If we are deficient in courage, no revisioning can occur. In a 1945 letter, speaking of the work of personal growth, Jung wrote:

The opus consists of three parts: insight, endurance, and action. Psychology is needed only in the first part, but in the second and third parts moral strength plays the predominant role.[1]

Many of us treat life as if it were a novel. We pass from page to page passively, assuming the author will tell us on the last page what it was all about. As Hemingway once said, if the hero does not die, the author just did not finish the story. So, on the last page we die, with or without illumination. The invitation of the Middle Passage is to become conscious, accept responsibility for the rest of the pages and risk the largeness of life to which we are summoned.

Wherever the reader may be in his or her life, the summons to us is the same as to Tennyson's Ulysses:

> The long day wanes: the slow moon climbs: the deep
> Moans round with many voices. Come, my friends,
> 'Tis not too late to seek a newer world.[2]

---

[1] *C.G. Jung Letters,* vol. 1, p. 375.

[2] "Ulysses," in Louis Untermeyer, ed., *A Concise Treasury of Great Poems,* p. 299.

1

The Provisional Personality

When I was in fifth grade, just after World War Two, our teacher bought some glass prisms which had been intended for submarine periscopes. Before and after class we would amuse ourselves by lurching down the aisles, running into walls and each other. We were fascinated by the question of reality and how to find one's way by such bent angles of sight. I wondered if those children who had to wear glasses all the time saw better or only different worlds. When I considered that the lens in our eyes also refracted the light, I had to wonder further whether the reality we saw might wholly depend on the lens through which we saw it.

It remains useful to borrow that youthful perception, to acknowledge that whatever reality may be, it will to some extent be shaped by the lens through which we see it. When we are born we are handed multiple lenses: genetic inheritance, gender, a specific culture and the variables of our family environment, all of which constitute our sense of reality. Looking back later, we have to admit that we have perhaps lived less from our true nature than from the vision of reality ordained by the lenses we used.

Therapists sometimes assemble a genogram which represents an emotional family tree. The history of the extended family over several generations reveals recurrent motifs. While genetic predispositions play their role, it is clear that families transmit their vision of life from generation to generation. The lens passes from parent to child, and out of that refracted perspective choices and consequences are repeated. And just as we see some aspects of the world through any given lens, so we will miss others.

Perhaps the first step in making the Middle Passage meaningful is to acknowledge the partiality of the lens we were given by family and culture, and through which we have made our choices and suffered their consequences. If we had been born of another time and place, to different parents who held different values, we would have had an entirely different lens. The lens we received generated a conditional life, which represents not who we are but how we were conditioned to see life and make choices. All generations are seduced into anthropocentrism, tending to defend their vision of the world as superior to that of others. So, too, we succumb to the belief

9

that the way we have grown to see the world is the only way to see it, the right way to see it, and we seldom suspect the conditioned nature of our perception.

Even in the most privileged of childhoods, life may be experienced as traumatic. We were connected to the heartbeat of the cosmos in our mother's womb. Suddenly we were thrust violently into the world to begin an exile and a search to recover the lost connectedness. Even religion (from Latin *religio,* "bond between man and the gods," or *religare,* "to bind back") may be seen as a projection of the search for lost connections onto the cosmos itself. For many, given the impact of poverty, hunger, abuses of various kinds, the initial experience of the world is devastating to their sense of self. As children they encapsulate affective, cognitive and sentient capacities to defend themselves against further hurt. They become the sociopaths and character disorders who fill our prisons and haunt our streets.

Sadly, for those thus devastated, the potential for growth and change is dismal; opening themselves to the world of pain, which growth requires, is too frightening. Most of us survive as merely neurotic, that is, split between the intrinsic nature of the child and the world to which we were socialized. We may even conclude that the unexamined adult personality is an assemblage of attitudes, behaviors and psychic reflexes occasioned by the traumata of childhood, whose primary purpose is the management of the level of distress experienced by the organic memory of childhood we carry within. This organic memory we may call the inner child, and our various neuroses represent strategies evolved unconsciously to defend that child. (The word "neurosis" is used here not in the clinical sense but rather as a generic term for the split between our nature and our acculturation.)

The nature of childhood wounding may be broadly generalized into two basic categories: 1) the experience of neglect or abandonment, and 2) the experience of being overwhelmed by life.

What we may call the provisional personality is a series of strategies, chosen by the fragile child to manage existential angst. Those behaviors and attitudes are typically assembled before age five and are elaborated in an astonishing range of strategic variations with a common motive—self-protection.

While external forces such as war, poverty or personal handicap play a large role in the child's perception of self and world, the primary influence on our lives derives from the character of the parent-child relationship. Anthropologists have described the cognitive processes of so-called primitive cultures and noted how they replicate our own childhood forms of thinking. Such cultures were characterized by animistic and magical thinking.

To the undifferentiated thinking of these cultures, and to childhood processing, the world is infused with soul-stuff; that is, the energies within and without are considered aspects of the same reality. This is animistic thinking. Further, such cultures inferred, as children do, that inner reality causes effects in the outer world and the outer causes the inner. Such is magical thinking. Like the primitive who could only know the limits of his own cave or rain forest, the child then attempts to read the environment in order to enhance comfort and further survival. (In Plato's famous parable the limit to human understanding is likened to the prisoners who draw conclusions about life based on the reflections they see on the cave walls to which they are chained.) The conclusions about the world drawn by the child are thus derived from a narrow spectrum and are inevitably partial and prejudicial. The child cannot say, "My parent has a problem, which has an effect upon me." The child can only conclude that life is anxious and the world unsafe.

In attempting to read the parent-child environment, the child interprets experience in three basic ways.

1) *The child phenomenologically interprets the tactile and emotional bonding, or lack thereof, as a statement about life in general.* Is it predictable and nurturing, or is it uncertain, painful and precarious? This primal perception then shapes the child's capacity to trust.

2) *The child internalizes specific behaviors of the parent as a statement about self.* Since the child can seldom objectify experience or perceive the inner reality of the parent, the parent's depression, anger or anxiety will be interpreted as a de facto statement about the child. "I am how I am viewed, or how I am treated," the child concludes. (A thirty-seven-year-old man asked his dying father, "Why were we never close?" The father launched into a tirade, "Do you remember when you were ten and you dropped your toy in the toilet and I had to work to get it out?" The list of trivial events continued. The son walked out of the hospital a free man. He had always thought himself unworthy of his father's love; his father freed him for a new self-image by revealing his craziness.)

3) *The child observes the behaviors of the adult's struggles with life and internalizes not only those behaviors but the attitudes they imply about self and world.* Thus, the child draws large conclusions about how to deal with the world. (One woman, exposed to her mother's omnipresent anxi-

ety, reported that she never began to question her mother's grim and foreboding outlook until she moved away to college. For the first year she assumed that the other students simply did not know how bad things were. By her sophomore year she began to suspect that she was a prisoner of her mother's anxiety and that she could begin to view herself and the world with a lighter heart.)

The conclusions about one's self and the world are clearly based on the very limited experience of a specific set of parents responding to particular issues. Such experience is overly personalized by the magical thought that "all of this experience is arranged for me and is about me"; the resulting conclusions are also overgeneralized, since one can only evaluate the unknown by what one has known thus far. With such a biased beginning, narrow and invariably prejudicial, one assembles perceptions, behaviors and reactions, marching into life with a partial vision.

The individual character of this flawed sense of self, and the strategies which are early elaborated into a personality, vary according to the nature of childhood experience. From each category of wounding—abandonment or feeling overwhelmed—a complex of behaviors evolves as an unconscious, reflexive response.[3]

When a child is overwhelmed, he or she experiences the immensity of the Other flooding across fragile boundaries. Lacking the power to choose other life circumstances, lacking even the objectivity to identify the nature of the problem as Other, and lacking the grounds for comparative experience, the child responds defensively, becoming hypersensitive to the environment and "choosing" passivity, codependence or compulsivity to protect fragile psychic territory. The child learns protean forms of accommodation, for life is seen as inherently overwhelming to a self that is relatively powerless. Thus a man, acting out his mother's incessant demand that he surpass his father and be a "success," became a highly skilled professional while slipping into spending habits that brought his life to financial and emotional bankruptcy. His adult life, seemingly the choice of a rational, free person, was a coerced compliance with the overwhelming pressure from that Other, coupled with an unconscious rebellion seeking failure as a

---

[3] We are talking here about experiences which may contribute to crisis in one's early sense of self. Thankfully, this is not the whole picture. There are generally also conditioned joys, allowing the possibility of, for instance, getting up in the morning in the belief that breakfast will be available, or that the day will offer possibilities for enlarged life.

passive-aggressive protest.

In the face of abandonment—that is, insufficient nurturing—the child may "choose" patterns of dependency and/or spend a lifetime in an addictive search for a more positive Other. Thus a woman who in childhood had experienced neglect later pursued one love partner after another, but always ended her relationships in disillusionment and frustration. In part her emotional neediness drove men away and in part she unconsciously chose emotionally remote men. Her father had been emotionally unavailable to her and her life reflexively formed around the dual, self-destructive perception of herself as "she who will not be given to and therefore deserves this," and the forlorn hope that the next man might redeem the parent-child wound within.

These wounds, and the various unconscious responses adopted by the inner child, become strong determinants of the adult personality. The child cannot incarnate a freely expressed personality; rather, childhood experience shapes his or her role in the world. Out of the wounding of childhood, then, the adult personality is less a series of choices than a reflexive response to the early experiences and traumata of life.

The Jungian model identifies any such reflexive, feeling-charged response with the nature of the personal complex. A complex is in itself neutral, though it carries an emotional charge associated with an experiential, internalized image. The greater the intensity of the initial experience, or the longer it was reiterated, the more power the complex has in one's life. Complexes are unavoidable because one has a personal history. The problem is not that we have complexes but that complexes have us. Some complexes are useful in protecting the human organism, but others interfere with choice and may even dominate a person's life.

Complexes are always more or less unconscious; they are charged with energy and operate autonomously. Although usually activated by an event in the present, the psyche operates analogously, saying in effect, "When have I been here before?" The current stimulus may be only remotely similar to something that happened in the past, but if the situation is emotionally analogous then the historically occasioned response is triggered. There are few who do not have an emotionally charged response around such issues as sex, money and authority because they are usually associated with important experiences in the past.

Of all the complexes, the most influential are those internalized experiences of parents we call the mother complex and the father complex. These are generally the two most important people we have ever encountered. They were there for the laying of the keel and the launching of the vessel. It was their treatment of us and their strategies toward life to which we were exposed. For example, Hemingway's macho heroes represented, among other things, the overcompensation by the child from Oak Park, Illinois, for the fear of women he acquired from a mother who wanted him to be a girl and who was emotionally seductive and invasive even when he reached adulthood. Franz Kafka was so dominated by his powerful father that he saw the universe itself as powerful, remote and indifferent. This is not to suggest that these and others have not created important art, for they surely have, but the form and private motive of their creativity was to work through, compensate for, and if possible transcend, the primal parent complexes.

So we all live out, unconsciously, reflexes assembled from the past. Even in early childhood, a growing split develops between our inherent nature and our socialized self. Wordsworth noted this two centuries ago when, in "Ode on Intimations of Immortality," he wrote:

> Heaven lies about us in our infancy!
> Shades of the prison-house begin to close
> Upon the growing boy, . . .
> At length the man perceives it die away,
> And fade into the light of common day.[4]

For Wordsworth, the socialization process was a progressive estrangement from the natural sense of self with which we are born. In Eugene O'Neill's play, *A Long Day's Journey Into Night,* the mother presents the case even more tragically:

> None of us can help the things life has done to us. They're done before you realize it. And once they're done, they make you do other things until at last everything comes between you and what you'd like to be, and you've lost your true self forever.[5]

The ancient Greeks perceived this split some twenty-five centuries ago. Their tragic figures were not evil, though they might sometimes commit evil deeds; they were persons bound to what they did not know about themselves. The *hamartia* (sometimes translated as "the tragic flaw," but I

---

[4] See Ernest Bernbaum, ed., *Anthology of Romanticism,* p. 232.

[5] *Complete Plays,* p. 212.

prefer "the wounded vision") represented the lens through which they made their choices. Out of the accumulation of unconscious forces and reflexive responses, choices were made and consequences followed. The tragic sense of life articulated in those grim dramas suggest that all of us, protagonists in our private dramas, may lead tragic lives. We can be driven by what we do not understand about ourselves. The liberating power of Greek tragedy was that through suffering the hero came to wisdom, that is, a revised relationship between inner truth (character) and outer truth (the gods or fate). Our lives are tragic only to the degree that we remain unconscious of both the role of the autonomous complexes and the growing divergence between our nature and our choices.

Most of the sense of crisis in midlife is occasioned by the pain of that split. The disparity between the inner sense of self and the acquired personality becomes so great that the suffering can no longer be suppressed or compensated. What psychologists call decompensation occurs. The person continues to operate out of the old attitudes and strategies, but they are no longer effective. Symptoms of midlife distress are in fact to be welcomed, for they represent not only an instinctually grounded self underneath the acquired personality but a powerful imperative for renewal.

The transit of the Middle Passage occurs in the fearsome clash between the acquired personality and the demands of the Self. A person going through such an experience will often panic and say, "I don't know who I am anymore." In effect, the person one has been is to be replaced by the person to be. The first must die. No wonder there is such enormous anxiety. One is summoned, psychologically, to die unto the old self so that the new might be born.

Such death and rebirth is not an end in itself; it is a passage. It is necessary to go through the Middle Passage to more nearly achieve one's potential and to earn the vitality and wisdom of mature aging. Thus, the Middle Passage represents a summons from within to move from the provisional life to true adulthood, from the false self to authenticity.

2

The Advent of the Middle Passage

The Middle Passage is a modern concept. Before the sudden extension of the life span around the turn of the century, life was, in Thomas Hobbes's words, "nasty, brutish, and short."[6] Changes in health care brought the average life expectancy into the forties at the beginning of our epoch. One has only to walk through the cemeteries of early America to see the lamentable rows of children who died when fevers passed through—the plague, ague, diphtheria, whooping cough, small pox and typhus, which modern children avoid through immunization. (I recall my city of about 100,000 being closed to all but essential transactions—no parks, no movies, no swimming—because of an outbreak of polio.)

Perhaps even more than limits on lifespan, those who survived to a later age were strongly controlled by the power of social institutions—church, family, social mores. (I had divorced persons pointed out to me in childhood, in the same tone as, "There goes a murderer.") Gender definitions were clear and absolute, injuring both women and men. Family and ethnic traditions offered the sense of roots, and sometimes community, but were also inbred and discouraged independence. A girl was expected to marry, raise a family, serve as the hub of the system which sustained and transmitted values. A boy was expected to grow up and take over his father's role, be the bread winner, but also support and endorse the continuity of values.

Many of these values were and remain laudable. But, given the weight of such institutional expectations, great spiritual violence was also suffered. One should not automatically applaud the fifty-year marriage without knowing what happened to the souls of those in the relationship. Perhaps they feared change, feared honesty and suffered. The child who lived up to the parent's expectations may have lost his or her soul along the way. Longevity and replication of values per se are not automatic virtues.

The idea that one is here to become oneself, that mysterious but absolutely unique being whose values may differ from kith and kin, was sel-

---

6 *Selections,* p. 106.

dom imparted to those who lived before our time. Even now some see it as a rather heretical notion. But the modern Zeitgeist is characterized most by the radical shift from the psychological power being vested in institutions to its relocation in the individual. More than any single change, meaning in the modern world has shifted from mace and miter to the individual. The great unifying ideologies have lost much of their psychic energy and have left modern individuals in a state of isolation. As Matthew Arnold observed a century and a half ago, we wander "between two worlds, one dead, the other powerless to be born."[7] For good or ill, the psychic gravity has shifted from institution to individual choice. Today there is a Middle Passage not only because people live long enough, but also because in Western society most now accept that we play the dominant role in shaping our own lives.

Tectonic Pressures and Seismic Intimations

As suggested earlier, the Middle Passage begins as a kind of tectonic pressure which builds from below. Like the plates of the earth which shift, rub against each other and accrue pressure that erupts as earthquakes, so the planes of the personality collide. The acquired sense of self, with its assembled perceptions and complexes, its defense of the child within, begins to grate and grind against the greater Self which seeks its own realization.

These seismic ripples may be dismissed by defensive ego-consciousness, yet the pressure builds. Invariably, long before one becomes conscious of a crisis the signs and symptoms have been there: depression which one outworks, overindulgence in alcohol, marijuana to enhance love-making, affairs, recurrent shifts in jobs, and so on—all efforts to override, ignore or outrun the underground pressures. From a therapeutic standpoint symptoms are to be welcomed, for they not only serve as arrows that point to the wound, they also show a healthy, self-regulating psyche at work.

Jung observed that a neurosis "must be understood, ultimately, as the suffering of a soul which has not discovered its meaning."[8] This does not suggest that one may achieve a life without suffering, but rather that the suffering is already upon us and one is obliged to find its meaning.

---

[7] *Poetry and Criticism of Matthew Arnold,* p. 187.

[8] "Psychotherapists or the Clergy," *Psychology and Religion: West and East,* CW 11, par. 497. [CW refers throughout to *The Collected Works of C.G. Jung]*

During World War Two the German theologian Dietrich Bonhoeffer went to a martyr's death for opposing Hitler. From Flensburg concentration camp he smuggled out a number of letters and papers. In one of them he struggled with the obvious question: Did God in some way bring about the camp and its horrible conditions? He realized that he could not answer such a question, but he wisely concluded that his task was to work with and through the horror to find the will of God in those circumstances.[9]

So one may say that in suffering the tectonic pressures of the psyche, one may not discover the ultimate purpose of life. But one is obliged to find the meaning of the conflict, that collision of selves which the Middle Passage entails. Out of this fated collision, this death-rebirth, new life emerges. One is invited to regain one's life, to live it more consciously, to wrest meaning from misery.

Awakening to the Middle Passage occurs when one is radically stunned into consciousness. I have seen many begin their Middle Passage when faced with a life-threatening illness or widowhood. To that point, even into the fifties and sixties, they had managed to remain unconscious, so dominated by complexes or collective values that the questions incarnated by the Middle Passage had been kept at bay. (Examples will be given in the next chapter.)

The Middle Passage is less a chronological event than a psychological experience. The two Greek words for "time," *chronos* and *kairos,* observe this distinction. *Chronos* is sequential, linear time; *kairos* is time revealed in its depth dimension. Thus, for an American, 1776 is more than a year on the calendar; it is a transcendent event that determines the quality of every subsequent year in the nation's history. The Middle Passage occurs when the person is obliged to view his or her life as something more than a linear succession of years. The longer one remains unconscious, which is quite easy to do in our culture, the more likely one is to see life only as a succession of moments leading toward some vague end, the purpose of which will become clear in due time. When one is stunned into consciousness, a vertical dimension, *kairos,* intersects the horizontal plane of life; one's life span is rendered in a depth perspective: "Who am I, then, and whither bound?"

The Middle Passage begins when the person is obliged to ask anew the question of meaning which once circumambulated the child's imagination

---

[9] *Letters and Papers from Prison,* p. 210.

but was effaced over the years. The Middle Passage begins when one is required to face issues which heretofore had been patched over. The question of identity returns and one can no longer evade responsibility for it. Again, the Middle Passage starts when we ask, "Who am I, apart from my history and the roles I have played?"

As we carry the history of our life in our psyche as a dynamic, autonomous presence, so we are likely to be defined and dominated by the past. As we have been conditioned to institutionalized roles, such as spouse, parent, wage-earner, so we have projected our identity onto those roles. Thus James Agee began his autobiographical novel: "We are talking now of summer evenings in Knoxville, Tennessee, in the time that I lived there so successfully disguised to myself as a child."[10] All the large questions were asked by the child we once were, as we observed the big folk silently, as we lay in our beds at night, half-fearful, half-joyous to be alive. But the weight of the schooling, the parenting and the acculturation process gradually replaces the child's sense of awe with normative expectations and cultural certainties. Agee concludes his preface by recalling how he was taken up to his bed by the big people, "as one familiar and well beloved in that home: but [they] will not, oh, will not, not now, not ever, but will not ever tell me who I am."[11]

Such questions, the large ones, give worth and dignity to our lives. If we forget them we are consigned to social conditioning, banality and finally despair. If we are fortunate to suffer enough, we are stunned into a reluctant consciousness and the questions return to us once again. If we are courageous enough, care enough about our lives, we may, through that suffering, get our lives back.

While some come to this fated meeting with themselves through a catastrophic event, all suffer warnings long before. The ground beneath one's feet trembles ever so slightly, and it is easy to ignore, at first. Seismic intimations, the big brothers of tectonic pressures, are always present before we become fully aware of them.

I know a man who by the time he was twenty-eight had achieved all he had hoped for—a doctorate, a family, a book published, a good teaching post. His first seismic intimations, acknowledged years later, were boredom and loss of energy. So he did what most do, more of the same. In the

---

[10] *A Death in the Family,* p.11.

[11] Ibid., p. 15.

next ten years he wrote more, had more children, taught in still better posts. All of this activity could be rationalized for it was outwardly productive and embodied the typical career ladder onto which we are prone to project our identity. When he was thirty-seven the growing underground depression broke through in full fury and he experienced near-complete enervation and loss of meaning. He quit his job, left his family and opened a Victorian ice-cream parlor in another city. Did he overcompensate for his previous life? Did he suppress the good and useful questions the Middle Passage was calling him to address? Or did he somehow hit upon the best way to spend his second half of life? Only time will tell, only he can say.

Often the seismic tremors occur as early as the late twenties, but they are easy to overlook then. Life is full; the road ahead beckons; rapid shifts, more effort, more energy are easy enough, and one overrides the warnings. One must have gone around a track a few times to even know if it is a circle or an oval. Patterns, with their costs and side-effects, can only be discerned as patterns when one has suffered them more than once. In retrospect, one is often chagrined, even humiliated, at the mistakes, the naivete, the projections. But such is the first adulthood: full of blunders, shyness, inhibitions, mistaken assumptions, and always, the silent rolling of the tapes of childhood. If one had not set forth and made those mistakes and crashed into those walls, then one would have remained a child. Reviewing one's life from the vantage-point of the second half requires understanding and forgiveness of the inevitable crime of unconsciousness. But not to become conscious in the second half is to commit an unforgivable crime.

There are a number of significant symptoms or experiences, detailed below, which signify the summons to the Middle Passage. They occur autonomously, outside the will of the ego. They transpire silently, day by day, and trouble the sleep of the inner child who wants the known and treasures security above all else. But they represent the ineluctable movement of life toward its unknown fulfillment, a teleological process which serves nature and its mysteries and cares little for the wishes of a nervous ego.

A New Kind of Thinking

As suggested earlier, childhood is characterized by magical thinking. The child's ego is not yet battle tested, not yet clear about boundaries. The objective, outer world and the inner, wishful world are often confused. Wishes seem possibilities, even probabilities. They represent the narcissism of the child who wants to believe he or she is the center of the cosmos. Such thinking is inflated and delusionary but in a child it is entirely healthy and wonderful. "I am going to grow up and wear white gowns and marry a prince." "I'm going to be an astronaut." "I'll be a famous rock star." (Try to recall your magical wishes of childhood and muse on what life did to them.) Most of all, the magical thinking of the child assumes, "I am immortal. I am not only going to be rich and famous, I am going to be sheltered from death and decline." This kind of thinking prevails until about the age of ten, though battered about the edges. The illusion of superiority, of specialness, takes some hard knocks when even other kids aren't impressed. (When I was a child I thought I might be the one to replace Joe Dimaggio in center field for the New York Yankees. Alas, the gods gave Mickey Mantle the necessary skills.)

Through the pain and confusion of adolescence, the magical thinking of the child suffers some rough wear. Yet the untested ego persists and exhibits what one might now call heroic thinking, characterized by greater realism, yes, but still with a considerable capacity for hope, for projection of the unknown through fantasies of grandeur and accomplishment. One may look at the sorry remains of a parent's marriage and conclude, "I know better than they and will choose wisely." One may still expect to be CEO, write the Great American Novel, be a terrific parent.

Heroic thinking is useful, for were one to suspect the trials and disappointments ahead, who would have set off into adulthood? I have yet to be asked to give a commencement address, but loathsome as such speeches usually are, I still might not have the heart to tell the truth. Who could bear to say to eager and hopeful faces, "In a few years you will likely hate your job, your marriage will be in peril, your kids will cause you fits, you may very well experience so much pain and confusion about your life that you will think of writing a book about it." Who could do that to the dewy-eyed, hitching their wagons to a star, even as they lurch down the same confused and wounding way their parents trod?

Heroic thinking, with its hopes and projections barely tempered by the world's ways, helps the young leave home and dive, as they must, into life. The youthful Wordsworth, across the channel and present at the start of the French revolution, wrote that to be young and to be there was very heaven.[12] A few years later he would despise how the revolutionary promise had been replaced by the Napoleonic regime. And the battle-weary

---

[12] "The Prelude," *Poetical Works of Wordsworth,* p. 570.

T.E. Lawrence saw his desert hopes sold out by the old men at the peace conferences. Still, youth sets off, as it must, falls, begins anew and blunders toward an appointment with time.

One is in the Middle Passage when the magical thinking of childhood and the heroic thinking of adolescence are no longer congruent with the life one has experienced. Those who have reached the mid-thirties and beyond have suffered an ample measure of disappointment and heartache to surpass even the shattered crushes of adolescence. Anyone in midlife has witnessed the collapsing of projections, of hopes and expectations, and has experienced the limitations of talent, intelligence, and, often, of courage itself.

Thus, the kind of thinking which characterizes the experience of the Middle Passage is rather prosaically called realistic. Realistic thinking gives us perspective. Greek tragedy demonstrated that the protagonist might be richer at the end, but in ruin, for he or she had come back into proper relationship with the gods. Shakespeare's King Lear was not a bad man; he was a fool, for he did not know what love was. His need for flattery deceived him; he paid through his flesh and his sanity and was the richer for it.

So life calls us all to a different perspective, a settling of the youthful hubris and inflation, and teaches the difference between hope and knowledge and wisdom. Hope is based on what might be. Knowledge is the valued lesson of experience. Wisdom is always humbling, never inflationary. Socrates' wisdom, for instance, was that he knew he knew nothing (but his "nothing" was so much more than the certainties of the sophists and savants of his day or ours).

The realistic thinking of midlife has as its necessary goal the righting of a balance, the restoration of the person to a humble but dignified relationship to the universe. A friend of mine once said he knew when the Middle Passage began for him. It came as a thought, a sentence in the head, the truth of which was self-evident. The thought was: "My life will never be the whole, only the parts." His psyche was announcing to him that the inflationary expectations of youth were not to be achieved. Such a realization may be felt by some as a defeat, but others will be moved to ask the next question, namely, "What work, then, needs to be done?"

Changes in Identity

Given the opportunity for a full life span, one passes through a series of different identities. It is the natural project of the ego to manage the existential anxiety of the person by stabilizing life as much as possible. But the nature of life clearly presumes and demands change. Approximately every seven to ten years there is a significant physical, social and psychological change in a person. Consider who you were at 14, at 21, at 28 and at 35, for example. While all of us are strung out along a continuum, we do have common passages to make. It is possible to generalize these cycles and identify a social and psychological agenda for each phase. While it is the hubristic assumption of the ego that it is in charge of life and that its vision will hold for the years to come, clearly there is an autonomous process, an ineluctable dialectic, which brings repeated deaths and rebirths. To acknowledge the inevitability of change, and to go with it, is a fine and necessary wisdom, but our natural tendency is to resist the dissolution of what we have managed to accomplish.[13]

The popularity of Gail Sheehy's *Passages* a few years ago testifies to the importance of the theme of periodic change. Yet, as Mircea Eliade, Joseph Campbell and other observers of the social and anthropological scene have suggested, our culture has lost the mythic road map which helps locate a person in a larger context. Without a tribal vision of the gods, and their spiritual network, modern individuals are cut adrift to wander without guidance, without models and without assistance through the various life stages. Thus, the Middle Passage, which calls for death before rebirth, is often experienced in frightening and isolating ways, for there are no rites of passage and little help from one's peers who are equally adrift.

As well as the many subphases of life, each a passage obliging death of some sort, there are four larger phases of life, each with a power to define the person's identity.

The first identity, childhood, is characterized most by the dependency of the ego on the actual world of the parents. Physical dependency is obvious, but the psychic dependency, wherein the child is identified with the family, is even greater. In ancient cultures adulthood began with the onset of puberty. No matter how geographically, culturally and ideologically varied the tribes, they all evolved meaningful rites of passage from the dependency of childhood to adult independence.

For all the disparity of initiatory practices, traditional rites of passage

---

[13] The unconscious will frequently acknowledge resistance and call for change in such dream images as a house being flooded or undermined, a car stolen or stalled, or one's purse or wallet, containing one's ID, stolen or lost. These images suggest that the old ego-state is becoming inadequate.

typically involved six stages. Briefly, they were 1) separation from the parents, often through a ritual kidnapping; 2) death, wherein childhood dependency is "killed"; 3) rebirth, wherein the new being, however nascent, is endowed; 4) the teachings, wherein the neophyte is told the primal myths of the tribe to give a sense of spiritual locus, the privileges and responsibilities in that particular tribe, and the knowledge of hunting, child-bearing, etc., necessary for adult functioning; 5) the ordeal, most commonly of further separation so that the initiate might learn there is a strength within to meet the task without; and finally 6) the return, whereby one reenters the community with the knowledge, mythic grounding and inner strength necessary to play a mature role. Often the initiate was even given a new name to befit the radical transformation.

What the rites of initiation hoped to achieve was separation from the parents, transmission of the sacred history of the tribe to provide spiritual grounding, and preparation for the responsibilities of adulthood. In our own culture there are no meaningful rites of passage into adulthood and thus many youth prolong their dependency. Our culture has become so heterogeneous, and has lost its mythic moorings in any case, that we can only transmit twentieth-century beliefs in materialism, hedonism and narcissism—with some computer skills thrown in. None of this provides salvation, connection to the earth and its great rhythms, meaning or depth to one's journey.

The second identity begins at puberty. But without the traditional rites of passage the young person is characterized by spiritual confusion and ego lability. The nascent ego is quite malleable and prey to the influence of peers and pop culture, both comprised of other confused adolescents. (Many therapists consider adolescence as extending roughly from age twelve to twenty-eight in North America. I came to conclude, after twenty-six years as a professor, that the primary cultural role of colleges was to serve as a holding tank while youth sought sufficient solidification of their egos to make a more substantive break from parental dependency. Indeed, much of their love and loathing for Mom and Dad was deflected to their Alma Mater.)

The second passage has as its primary task, then, the solidification of the ego through which the youth gains sufficient strength to leave parents, go out into the larger world, and struggle for survival and the achievement of desire. Such a person has to say to the world: "Hire me. Marry me. Trust me." And then prove worthy. Sometimes at midlife one still has not taken the decisive steps away from dependency and into the world. Some may still be living with parents. Some may lack the personal strength and self-worth necessary to risk relationship. Others may have failed to meet the tasks of work with sufficient strength and resolve. For those persons, the body may have reached midlife chronologically, but their *kairos* is still childhood.

I call the period from roughly twelve to forty the first adulthood. The young person who knows, deep down, that he or she lacks a clear sense of self can only try to act like the other big people. It is an understandable delusion that if one comports oneself as one's parents have, or rebels against their example, one will thereby be an adult. If one holds a job, marries, becomes a parent and taxpayer, the confirmation of adulthood will surely follow. In fact, what has occurred is that the dependency of childhood has partly gone underground and has been projected onto the roles of adulthood. These roles are not unlike parallel tunnels. Out of the confusion of adolescence one walks through them with the assumption that they will confirm one's identity, provide fulfillment and still the terrors of the unknown. The first adulthood, which may in fact extend throughout one's life, is a provisional existence, lacking the depth and uniqueness which makes that person truly an individual.

These tunnels are of indeterminate length. They endure for as long as the projected identity and dependency upon them still seems to work. It is next to impossible to tell a thirty year old who is productively working, married and expecting a second child that he or she is still in a form of extended childhood. The parent complexes and the authority of the roles offered by society have sufficient power to attract the projections of anyone still exploring life in the world. As suggested earlier, the Self, that mysterious process within each of us which summons us to ourselves, often expresses itself through symptoms—loss of energy, depression, sudden fits of rage or over-consumption—but the power of the projections is such that one may keep the larger questions of the journey at bay. How terrifying it is, then, when the projections wear off and the person can no longer avoid the insurgence of the Self. Then, one must confess to powerlessness, to loss of control. The ego never was in control but rather was driven by the energy of the parental and collective complexes, sustained by the power of the projections onto the roles offered by the culture to those who would be adults. As long as the roles have normative power, as long as the projections work, the individual has managed to forestall the appointment with the inherent Self.

The third phase of identity, the second adulthood, is launched when one's projections have dissolved. The sense of betrayal, of failed expectations, the vacuum and loss of meaning which occur with this dissolution, creates the midlife crisis. It is in this crisis, however, that one has the chance to become an individual—beyond the determinism of parents, parent complexes and cultural conditioning. Tragically, the regressive power of the psyche, with its reliance on authority, often keeps a person in thrall to these complexes and thereby freezes development. In working with the elderly, each of whom has to face loss and anticipate death, there are clearly two categories. There are those for whom the life remaining is still a challenge, still worthy of the good fight, and those for whom life is full of bitterness, regret and fear. The former are invariably those who have gone through some earlier struggle, experienced the death of the first adulthood and accepted greater responsibility for their lives. They spend their last years living more consciously. Those who avoided the first death are haunted by the second, afraid their lives have not been meaningful.

Characteristics of the second adulthood will be discussed more fully in later chapters. But it is important to note here that it is only attainable when the provisional identities have been discarded and the false self has died. The pain of such loss may be compensated by the rewards of the new life which follows, but the person in the midst of the Middle Passage may only feel the dying. The fourth identity, mortality, which involves learning to live with the mystery of death, will also be discussed later, but already in the second adulthood it is essential to accept the reality of death.

The good news which follows the death of the first adulthood is that one may reclaim one's life. There is a second shot at what was left behind in the pristine moments of childhood. The good news deriving from our confrontation with death is that our choices really do matter and that our dignity and depth derive precisely from what Heidegger called "the Being-toward-Death."[14] Heidegger's definition of our ontological condition is not morbid but rather a recognition of the teleological purposes of nature, the birth-death dialectic.

Another way to look at these shifting identities is to classify their different axes. In the first identity, childhood, the operative axis is the parent-child relationship. In the first adulthood the axis lies between ego and

---

[14] *Being and Time,* p. 97.

world. The ego, one's conscious being, struggles to project itself into the world and create a world within the world. Childhood dependency has been driven into the unconscious and/or projected onto various roles, and one is primarily oriented to the outer world. In the second adulthood, during and after the Middle Passage, the axis connects ego and Self. It is natural for consciousness to assume that it knows all and is running the show. When its hegemony is overthrown, the humbled ego then begins the dialogue with the Self. The Self may be defined as the teleological purposiveness of the organism. This is a mystery larger than we will ever understand and its unfolding will provide us with more magnificence than our short lifetime can possibly incarnate.

The fourth axis is Self-God, or Self-Cosmos if one prefers. This axis is framed by the cosmic mystery which transcends the mystery of individual incarnation. Without some relationship to the cosmic drama, we are constrained to lives of transience, superficiality and aridity. Since the culture most of us have inherited offers little mythic mediation for the placement of self in a larger context, it is all the more imperative that the individual enlarge his or her vision.

These shifting axes delineate the sea-changes of the soul. When we are swept from one axis to the next without our volition, then confusion, even terror, may ensue. But the nature of our humanity seems to oblige each of us to move toward a larger and larger role in the great drama.

Withdrawal of Projections

Projection is a fundamental mechanism of the psyche, a strategy derived from the fact that what is unconscious is projected. (The word "projection" comes from the Latin *pro + jacere*, "to throw before.") Jung has written that "the general psychological reason for projection is always an activated unconscious that seeks expression."[15] Elsewhere he states: "Projection is never made; it happens, it is simply there. In the darkness of anything external to me I find, without recognizing it as such, an interior or psychic life that is my own."[16]

In the face of the awesome outer world and the unknown immensity of the inner, our natural tendency is to project our anxiety onto the parent, whom we believe to be omniscient and omnipotent. When we are obliged

---

[15] "The Symbolic Life," *The Symbolic Life,* CW 18, par. 352.
[16] *Psychology and Alchemy,* CW 12, par. 346.

to leave our parents we tend to project knowledge and power onto institutions, persons in authority and socialized roles (the tunnels mentioned above). We assume that to act like the big people is to become one. Youth setting out on the first adulthood cannot know then that the big people are often children in big bodies and big roles. Some of them may even believe they *are* their roles. Those less inflated are more conscious of their uncertainties, while those in the Middle Passage and beyond are experiencing the dissolution of their projections.

Of the many projections possible, the most common are those onto the institutions of marriage, parenting and career. More will be said later of the role of projection in marriage, but perhaps no other social construct has so much unconscious baggage imposed upon it. Few at the altar are conscious of the enormity of their expectations. No one would speak aloud the immense hopes: "I am counting on you to make my life meaningful." "I am counting on you to always be there for me." "I am counting on you to read my mind and anticipate all my needs." "I am counting on you to bind my wounds and fulfill the deficits of my life." "I am counting on you to complete me, to make me a whole person, to heal my stricken soul." Just as the truth cannot be told in a commencement address, so the hidden agenda may not be spoken at the altar. One would be too embarrassed, if one acknowledged them, by the impossibility of these demands. Most marriages which end are broken by the weight of such expectations and those which persist are often badly scarred. Romance feeds on the distant, the imagined, the projected; marriage sups the common gruel of propinquity, ubiquity and commonality.

In his book *He*, Robert Johnson suggests that most moderns, no longer at home in the old mythic systems, have transferred the needs of the soul to romantic love.[17] Indeed, images of the beloved are carried within each of us from childhood and projected onto one who can receive our unconscious material. As the Persian poet Rumi wrote:

> The moment I heard my first love story I started looking for you,
>   not knowing how blind that was.
> Lovers don't finally meet somewhere.
> They're in each other all along.[18]

Living with another person on a daily basis automatically wears away

---

[17] *He*, pp. 82-83.
[18] See Sam Kean and Anne Valley-Fox, *Your Mythic Journey*, p. 26.

projections. This person to whom one has delivered one's soul, to whom one has opened up in intimacy, turns out to be only a mortal like us, afraid, needy and also projecting heavy expectations. Intimate relationships of any kind carry such a large freight because they come closest to replicating that Intimate Other which once was the parent. We do not wish to think of our partner as a parent. We spent so much energy getting away from parents, after all. But the beloved becomes that Intimate Other, onto whom the same needs and dynamics are projected, to the degree that we are unconscious. It is not surprising, then, that people end up choosing someone as like or as unlike their parents as they can, for the simple reason that the parent complexes have a hand in the choice all along. When the Biblical peoples declared that marriage required leaving mother and father,[19] it was harder than even they imagined. Thus, the withdrawal of the projections of nurturance, empowerment and healing which one brings to the Intimate Other can only partially be achieved. The discrepancy between silent hope and quotidian reality causes pain of considerable magnitude during the Middle Passage.

Another role which receives heavy identity projections is parenthood. Most of us believe we are capable of knowing what is right for our child. We are certain we can avoid the mistakes our parents made. But inevitably we all are guilty of projecting our unlived lives onto our children. Jung observed that the largest burden a child must bear is the unlived life of the parents. The Stage-Door Mother and the Little-League father are stereotypes, but just as insidious are the jealousies a parent can have of a child's success. Thus a constant stream of messages, overt and covert, bombard a child. The child will carry the angers and hurts of the parent and suffer the full range of manipulations and coercions. Worst of all, we may unconsciously expect that child to make us happy with ourselves, to fulfill our lives and to bring us to a higher place.

By the time we come to the Middle Passage, our children have arrived at their adolescence and, pimply, sullen, rebellious and generally as obnoxious as we were to our parents, they resist our projections with a fury. If we realize how difficult and dangerous the parent complexes are as obstacles to the individual's journey toward personhood, we know those adolescents are right to resist the demand to be extensions of their parents. Nevertheless, the gap between the expectations of parenthood and the

---

[19] Mark 10: 7-8..

frictions of family life cause further pain to those in the Middle Passage. The disappointment can only be assuaged if one remembers what one wished one's own parents had known, that the child only passes through our bodies and our lives en route to the mystery of his or her own life. When the parent at midlife can accept this, the ambivalence of parenting gains its proper perspective.

Freud believed that work and love were the prime requisites for sanity. Our work represents a very large occasion for meaning or for its denial. If, as Thoreau suggested long ago, most people lead lives of quiet desperation,[20] then surely one reason is that work for so many is demeaning and demoralizing. Even those who have achieved the positions to which they aspired will often find themselves strangely afflicted with ennui. I knew too many students who became business majors or computer programmers because their parents, or that parent substitute, the amorphous society, seemed to demand it. Both those who achieve what they desire, and those pressured to fill someone else's need, often grow bored by their careers. For every aspirant on the career ladder, there is a burned-out executive who longs for a different life.

One's career, like marriage and parenting, is a prime vehicle for the projection of 1) identity, which is thought to be confirmed through the visible mastery of a body of expertise; 2) nurturance, that one will be fed by being productive; and 3) transcendence, that one will overcome the pettiness of the spirit through successive achievements. When these projections dissolve, and the dissatisfaction with how one is using one's life energy can no longer be displaced, then one is in the Middle Passage.

The more traditional the marriage, the more fixed the gender roles, the more likely the partners will find themselves drawn in opposite directions. He has been to the mountain top and all one can see from there is a corporate parking lot. He would gladly throttle back or retire. She, having devoted herself to family life, feels cheated, unappreciated and underdeveloped, and wants to go back to school or find renewing work. For men, the issue of work at midlife often occasions depression, the deflation of hope and ambition. Women starting over often experience anxiety regarding their level of competence or ability to compete. Again, there is bad news, good news, and more. The bad news is that each has exhausted a major area of projected identity and wishes a new start. The good news is that out of

---

[20] *The Best of Walden and Civil Disobedience,* p. 15.

such dissatisfaction genuine renewal can come and another facet of the individual's potential may be tapped for everyone's gain. More bad news is that one projection may only be traded for another; but even so, one draws closer toward that appointment with one's Self. If a spouse feels threatened by change, and resists, then he or she can be assured of living with an angry and depressed partner. In the crucible of marriage change will not inevitably be for the better, but it will be inevitable. Otherwise the marriage may not survive, especially if it hinders the growth of either partner.

Still another projection which must be dissolved at midlife has to do with the role of the parent as symbolic protector. Usually by midlife one's parents are declining in their powers or deceased. Even when the parental relationship has been troubled or distant, the parent is still symbolically present to provide an invisible psychic barrier. As long as the parental figure is alive, a psychic buffer against the unknowable and dangerous universe survives. When it is removed, one often feels the whiff of existential anxiety. One client, in her early forties, suffered panic attacks when her mid-seventies parents decided, amicably, to divorce. Their marriage had never been good, she knew, but it still served her as an invisible shield against that large universe. Even before their mortal removal, the divorce shattered the invisible protection—one more way to feel alone and abandoned at midlife.

While there are many other sorts of projections which fail to survive the first adulthood, the loss of expectations regarding marriage, children, career and the parent as protector are the most telling.

In *Projection and Re-Collection in Jungian Psychology,* Marie-Louise von Franz notes five stages of projection.[21] First, the person is convinced that the inner (that is, unconscious) experience is truly outer. Second, there is a gradual recognition of the discrepancy between the reality and the projected image (one falls out of love, for example). Third, one is required to acknowledge this discrepancy. Fourth, one is driven to conclude one was somehow in error originally. And, fifth, one must search for the origin of the projected energy within oneself. This last stage, the search for the meaning of the projection, always involves a search for a greater knowledge of oneself.

The erosion of projections, the withdrawal of the hopes and expectations they embody, is almost always painful. But it is a necessary

---

[21] *Projection and Re-Collection in Jungian Psychology,* pp. 9ff.

prerequisite for self-knowledge. The loss of hope that the outer will save us occasions the possibility that we shall have to save ourselves. For every inner child, riddled with fear and looking for rescue from the adult world, there is an adult potentially able to take responsibility for that child. By rendering the contents of the projections conscious, one has taken a large step toward emancipation from childhood.

Changes in the Body and Sense of Time

The general attitude of the first adulthood is to project one's sense of youthful inflation onto the indeterminate future. When energy flags it is easy enough to dismiss the event. Perhaps one did not get enough sleep the night before. Then one finds oneself performing as before, but not re-bounding as quickly. Then the minor aches and strains persist.

Youth generally takes the body for granted. It will be there to serve and protect and may be drawn deeply upon when needed, always replenishing itself. But a day comes when one realizes that, again, there is an in-eluctable transformation occurring beyond one's will. The body becomes the enemy, reluctant antagonist in the heroic drama in which we have cast ourselves. The hopes of the heart persist, but the body will no longer re-spond as once it did. As Yeats lamented, "Consume my heart away; sick with desire / and fastened to a dying animal."[22] What once was the humble servant of the ego now becomes a surly opponent; one feels trapped in the body. However high the spirit wishes to soar, what Alfred North Whitehead called "the withness of the body"[23] calls one back to earth.

So too, time, which once seemed the arena for endless play, the far field of ever-returning light, also becomes a trap. The shift, a sudden *peripeteia*, leads one to recognize not only that one is mortal, that there is an end, but that there is no way one will ever accomplish all that the heart longs for and pursues. "Only the parts, never the whole," my friend concluded. The graceful body, a charnel house; the endless summer, a spin into darkness— it is this sense of limit and incompleteness which calls the first adulthood to an end. Dylan Thomas wrote of this transit in hauntingly beautiful lines:

> Nothing I cared, in the lamb white days, that time would take me
> Up to the swallow-thronged loft by the shadow of my hand,

---

[22] *The Collected Poems of W.B. Yeats,* p. 191.
[23] *Nature and Life,* p. 126.

In the moon that is always rising,
    Nor that riding to sleep
I should hear him fly with the high fields
And wake to the farm forever fled from the childless land.
Oh as I was young and easy in the mercy of his means,
    Time held me green and dying
Though I sang in my chains like the sea.[24]

The Diminution of Hope

When the purse strings of the heart suddenly tighten, and one knows oneself mortal, the limitations of our lives are suddenly inescapable. The magical thinking of childhood, and the heroic thinking of that extended adolescence called the first adulthood, prove inadequate to the realities of life. The expansionist, imperial ego deflects the insecurities of childhood into a grandiosity. "Fame: I'm going to live forever; I'm going to learn how to fly." The hopes of the nascent ego for immortality and celebrity are in direct proportion to childhood fear and ignorance of the world. Similarly, the bitterness and depression of midlife is linked to the amount of energy invested in the phantasmal wishes of childhood.

The ego needs to establish a foothold in a large and unknowable universe. Not unlike the coral atoll which is formed by accreting skeletal shards, so the ego collects experiential fragments and builds them as a structure to hold fast in the great tidal shifts. Naturally, ego consciousness concludes that it must defend against the overwhelming experiences of life and compensate its insecurities by grandiosity. In our insecurity, the delusion of greatness serves to keep the darkness at bay while we drift off to sleep at night. But to flounder amid ordinariness is the sour leaven of midlife. And even those who gain renown, who name hotels after themselves, who drive their children to madness, are no more exempt than the rest of us from the encounter with limit, with deflation and with mortality. If the accouterments of power and privilege gave peace or meaning, or even lasting satisfaction, then there would be some substance to the infantile wishes we project.

Another ego-related hope of youth is the desire for the perfect relationship. While one has seen less than perfect relationships all around, we are

---

[24] "Fern Hill," in *Collected Poems,* p. 180.

prone to assume we are somehow wiser, better able to choose, better equipped to avoid the pitfalls. The Koran warns, "Do you think that you shall enter the Garden of Bliss without such trials as came to those who passed before you?"[25] We imagine such advice applies to others. While more will be written later on this subject, the second greatest deflation of midlife expectations is the encounter with the limitations of relationships. The Intimate Other who will meet our needs, take care of us, always be there for us, is seen to be an ordinary person, like ourselves, also needy, and projecting much the same expectations onto us. Marriages often end at midlife and one central reason is the enormity of childhood hopes which are imposed upon the fragile structure between two people. Others will not and cannot meet the grandiose needs of the inner child and so we are left feeling abandoned and betrayed.

Projections embody what is unclaimed or unknown within ourselves. Life has a way of dissolving projections and one must, amid the disappointment and desolation, begin to take on the responsibility for one's own satisfaction. There is no one out there to save us, to take care of us, to heal the hurt. But there is a very fine person within, one we barely know, ready and willing to be our constant companion. Only when one has acknowledged the deflation of the hopes and expectations of childhood and accepted direct responsibility for finding meaning for oneself, can the second adulthood begin.

I knew a man who acknowledged his core issue to be envy. By definition, envy is the perception that someone else has what one hungers for. While this man had suffered genuine deprivations in childhood, he was still defining himself negatively—"I am that absence which sees its fullness in some other." Recognizing that childhood cannot be relived and its history reversed, that no one will magically fill the void within, is surely painful, but then begins the possible path to healing. What is so difficult is to trust that one's own psyche will prove sufficient to heal itself. Sooner or later, that leap into trusting one's own resources must occur or one continues the futile pursuit of of childhood fantasies. Letting go of those will-of-the-wisps of immortality, perfection and grandiosity does much to poison a person's spirit and relationships. In the experience of estrangement from self and others, however, is the potential for that solitude wherein one may discern the largeness of the person within.

---

[25] Cited in Joseph Campbell, *The Power of Myth,* p. 126.

The Experience of Neurosis

Just as romantic love may be seen as a transient madness in which people make decisions for eternity based on the emotions of the moment, so the turbulence of the Middle Passage may resemble a psychotic break wherein the person acts "crazy" or withdraws from others. If we realize that the assumptions by which the person has lived his or her life are collapsing, that the assembled strategies of the provisional personality are decompensating, that a world-view is falling apart, then the thrashing about is understandable. In fact, one might even conclude that there is no such thing as a crazy act if one understands the emotional context. Emotions are not chosen; they choose us and have a logic of their own.

A client in a psychiatric facility repeatedly threw chairs through windows. It was assumed that he wished to escape and he was placed in restraints. Under careful questioning, however, it came out that he believed the air was being pumped out of his room and he needed to breathe fresh air. His sense of psychic enclosure had converted symbolically into claustrophobia. His desire for more air was logical, given the emotional premise. When moved to more commodious quarters, he felt secure. His behavior was not crazy. He was logically acting out the psychological experience of enclosure and suffocation.

So, during the Middle Passage, when the largeness of emotion breaks through ego boundaries, we often concretize what is symbolically injured or neglected. The man who runs away with his secretary is terrified that his inner life, his lost feminine dimension, will wither and disappear forever. As this need is largely unconscious, he projects that missing woman within upon the woman without. The woman who suffers a depression is turning her unwelcome anger within, upon the only person she has permission to attack. Neither is crazy though they may suffer such judgments from others. Both are responding to the enormity of the needs and emotions which beset them just at a time when their maps of reality no longer match the terrain.

There is an excellent example of meaningful madness in the short story "Eli, the Fanatic," by Philip Roth.[26] Set just after World War Two, when the world was flooded with displaced persons, Eli is an established lawyer in suburban America. When a group of survivors from a concentration

---

[26] See *Goodbye, Columbus and Five Short Stories.*

camp are relocated in his town, Eli is sent to ask them to tone down their ethnic identity. In turn, he is confronted with the emptiness of his own identity and his shallow link to his heritage. Ultimately he trades his Brooks Brothers suit for the shabby attire of the old Rabbi and walks down the main street of his town chanting his Biblical name. The final scene of the story depicts his incarceration and injection with a powerful tranquilizer. He is judged mad when in fact he has simply discarded his provisional identity, shed the trappings and projections of the upwardly mobile, and relocated himself within an ancient tradition. As his new identity is not congruent with the accepted matrix, he is deemed "crazy" and his new consciousness is medicated. One might say of him as Wordsworth said of Blake, "There are some who think this man mad, but I prefer the madness of this man to the sanity of others."[27]

The experience of the widening gap between the acquired sense of self, with all its attendant strategies and projections, and the demands of the Self which lies buried beneath one's history, is known to all, for all feel separated from themselves. The word "neurosis," coined by the Scottish physician Cullen in the late eighteenth century, suggests that what we are experiencing is neurological. But neurosis, or a so-called nervous breakdown, has nothing to do with neurology. It is simply the term used to describe the intrapsychic division, and subsequent protest, of the psyche. All of us are neurotic because we experience a split between what we are and what we are meant to be. The symptomatic protest of the neurosis, expressed in depression, substance abuse or destructive behavior, is denied as long as possible. But symptoms gather energy anew and begin to operate autonomously, outside the volition of the ego. It is as useless to tell a dieting person not to be hungry as to ask a symptom to go away. The symptom, even when counterproductive, is meaningful, for it expresses in symbolic form what is longing for expression.

What the frightened individual wishes above all is the restoration of the sense of self which once worked. What the therapist knows is that the symptoms are helpful clues to the place of injury or neglect, pointing the way to subsequent healing. The therapist also knows that the experience of midlife neurosis, when it can be faced, constitutes an enormous opening to transformation. As Jung asserted, "The outbreak of the neurosis is not just a matter of chance. As a rule it is most critical. It is usually the moment

---

[27] Martin Price, *To the Palace of Wisdom,* p. 432.

when a new psychological adjustment, a new adaptation is demanded."[28] This implies that our own psyche has organized this crisis, produced this suffering, precisely because injury has been done and change must occur.

I am frequently reminded of the dream of a woman who first came into analysis when she was sixty-five, just after the death of her husband. She had grown up with a very strong, very positive father relationship and had a powerful father complex. Her husband was several years older than she. Naturally, she was devastated by the loss of both through death. She sought solace from a cleric who suggested that she enter therapy. Initially, she thought therapy would take away her pain. Predictably, she projected considerable authority onto the therapist.

Several months into the analysis she had a dream in which she and her deceased husband were on a journey together. When they reached a stream with a bridge, she realized she had forgotten her purse. Her husband went ahead and she returned to fetch her purse. She retraced her steps and, upon arriving at the same bridge, was joined from the left by an unknown man who crossed over the bridge with her. She explained to this man that her husband was ahead of her but that he also had died. "I'm so alone, so alone," she lamented. "I know," the stranger replied, "but it has been good for me."

In the dream, and in reporting it later, the dreamer was angry at the stranger for his seeming insensitivity to her bereavement. I was excited by this dream for it showed a definite psychological shift. While her father and husband were in fact deceased, they continued to have a dominating role in her definition of herself. The father complex, seemingly benign, had constituted an external authority, blocking her from finding her own. The bridge constituted the capacity to make the transition from outer to inner authority. And the unknown stranger represented her inner masculine principle, the animus, which had lain undeveloped because of the power of the father complex. It is a good example of the wonderful, self-regulating wisdom of the psyche; the suffering of her ego had occasioned the growth of an inner component not under the domination of the father. Her Middle Passage began, then, at age sixty-five, when she embarked on a journey to claim her own identity and find her own authority, both requisites for adulthood.

---

[28] "Psychoanalysis and Neurosis," *Freud and Psychoanalysis,* CW 4, par. 563.

Another way to look at neurosis is to consider that the suffering arises out of a considerable degree of dissociation. In the process of responding to the socialization process of childhood and the pressure of outer realities, we become progressively estranged from ourselves. Protests from within are squelched by the weight of the outer world. But by midlife the injury and neglect to the soul may be such that parts of the psyche strenuously resist further insult. This resistance manifests in symptoms. Rather than medicate their message away, we must engage them in dialogue to bring about that "new adaptation" referred to above by Jung.

It is a very difficult truth to those in immense suffering, in the dark night of the soul, that their pain is good for them, as the above dreamer's mystery man said. But the way ahead may be found in the suffering. There is no cure, for life is not a disease, nor death a punishment. But there is a path to more meaningful, more abundant life.

I recall a woman with a history of great suffering, beginning with a turbulent passage into life and a malformed body, periods of neglect and abandonment, and a series of dependent and humiliating relationships. At midlife her world tumbled and she went inward to find the person she never knew. The word she used to describe the ordeal of the Middle Passage was "fragmentation." Many have suffered such fragmentation and many, understandably, flee to some defended stronghold of neurosis and hunker down before the winds of change. But when I asked this woman what she did when she felt fragmented, who she was during this painful process, she answered in terms which told me clearly that she would make it through to a more authentic life. She said, as best I recall, "I talk to this part of me, and then I listen. And I talk to that part and I listen. And I try to learn what Psyche wants of me."

She spoke of Psyche as a living presence, a feminine knowing which would direct her. Some would say, "She's hearing voices; she's schizophrenic." Quite the contrary. We all hear voices, so to speak; that is what complexes are—parts of ourselves that speak to us, and we, not hearing consciously, become their prisoner. This woman was assisting the dialogue between ego and Self, the dialogue which can heal the split history has wrought. Her ability to trust that inner process is as necessary as it is rare. Nature is not against us. The poet Rilke beautifully observed that our inner dragons may actually seek our assistance:

> How should we be able to forget those ancient myths that are at the
> beginning of all peoples, the myths about dragons that at the last

moment turn into princesses; perhaps all the dragons of our lives are
princesses who are only waiting to see us once beautiful and brave.
Perhaps everything terrible is in its deepest being something helpless
that wants help from us.[29]

Giving attentive help transforms these dragons into sources of energy for
renewal.

Recall Jung's definition of neurosis as "suffering which has not discovered its meaning."[30] Indeed, suffering seems to be a prerequisite for the
transformation of consciousness. Elsewhere Jung suggests that neurosis is
"inauthentic suffering."[31] Authentic suffering requires encounters with
dragons. Inauthentic suffering implies flight from them.

If Jung and Rilke are right, and I think they are, our dragons represent
all that we fear and which threatens to swallow us; but they are also neglected parts of ourselves which may prove immensely valuable. In being
taken seriously, even loved by us, they will respond by providing enormous energy and meaning for the journey of the second half of life.

---

[29] *Letters to a Young Poet,* p. 69.

[30] See above, note 8.

[31] "The Significance of the Unconscious in Individual Education," *The Development of Personality,* CW 17, par. 154.

3

The Turn Within

The central project of the first half of life is to build ego identity. Everyone knows someone who never really left home. Sometimes the person literally lives with Mom or Dad and takes care of them; one may live across the street, or in the same community, or even a thousand miles away and still be under their thumb. The person who has not separated psychologically from the parents is still tied to them. The project of the first half of life is incomplete.

An insufficiently attained ego identity haunts and hinders a person's development in the second half of life. Readiness for the second adulthood requires more than a geographical separation from the parents. One must have found a way to be productive with one's energy. This does not mean simply holding a paying job; it means that one feels challenged by a task and productive in its fulfillment.

There must also be a mature commitment to relationship. The inability to meet another half way, to hold one's own in the inevitable friction of relationships, represents a primary failure to achieve a sense of one's own psychic reality. Further, there should also be some engagement as a citizen in the outer world. Each of us has had moments when we would like to withdraw from the world's lunacy, and occasional withdrawal can surely be restorative to the soul. But to flee forever is to shun the further development of personal identity. Again, Jung has expressed this task eloquently:

> The natural course of life demands that the young person should sacrifice his childhood and his childish dependence on the physical parents, lest he remain caught body and soul in the bonds of unconscious incest.[32]

> Fear is a challenge and a task, because only boldness can deliver from fear. And if the risk is not taken, the meaning of life is somehow violated, and the whole future is condemned to a hopeless staleness, to a drab grey lit only by will-o'-the-wisps.[33]

---

[32] *Symbols of Transformation,* CW 5, par. 553.
[33] Ibid., par. 551.

As we have seen, even the successfully attained ego identity can be undermined at midlife. The heartbreak of a failed relationship, the disaffection from those who were to support and save us, the loss of enthusiasm for the career ladder—all represent the erosion of ego projections and the sense of identity hitherto sustained by them. However successful one may have been in consolidating the ego state, in building a world of one's own, the deflations of the Middle Passage are experienced as confusion, frustration and loss of identity.

Often, when one is embarked on the Middle Passage, the unfinished business of the first half of life becomes painfully apparent. For example, in losing a marriage one may come face to face with the tacit dependency that marriage concealed. One may realize that one had projected the parent complex onto the spouse, or that one has no work skills or confidence. Then the chickens of the first half come home to roost, creating resentment and the desire to blame someone.

One of the most powerful shocks of the Middle Passage is the collapse of our tacit contract with the universe—the assumption that if we act correctly, if we are of good heart and good intentions, things will work out. We assume a reciprocity with the universe. If we do our part, the universe will comply. Many ancient stories, including the Book of Job, painfully reveal the fact that there is no such contract, and everyone who goes through the Middle Passage is made aware of it. No one sets out upon the marital barque, for example, without high hopes and good intentions, however uncertain the compass and shifting the tides. When one stands amid the rubble of a partnership, then one has not only lost the relationship, but also, often, a whole world-view.

Perhaps the greatest shock of all is the erosion of the illusion of ego supremacy. However successful our ego project may once have been, it can hold dominion no longer. The breakdown of the ego means that one is not really in control of life. Nietzsche once noted how dismayed humans are when they discover that they are not God. It's enough to realize that one is not even able to manage one's own life very well. Jung emphasized the shudder which occurs when we find we are not masters in our own house. Thus, apart from shock, confusion, even panic, the fundamental result of the Middle Passage is to be humbled. With Job we sit atop the dung heap, bereft of illusion, and wonder where it all went wrong. Yet out of this experience may come new life. The strength one has acquired in the struggle of the first half may now be called upon for the encounter with the second.

If we have no ego strength, we are unable to effect that shift from the ego-world axis to ego-Self. What was left undone in ego separation and solidification remains as an obstacle to the growth of the person to be.

Life is unsparing in asking us to grow up and take responsibility for our lives. As simplistic as it may sound, growing up is really the inescapable demand of the Middle Passage. It means finally confronting one's dependencies, complexes and fears without the mediation of others. It requires us to relinquish blaming others for our lot and to take full responsibility for our physical, emotional and spiritual well-being. My own analyst once said to me, "You must make your fears your agenda." It was a formidable prospect, but I knew the truth of his assertion. That agenda was calling me to account and it would take all the strength I could muster.

During the Middle Passage, we often still have obligations to children, economic reality, the demands of duty. Yet even while the outer world continues to require our efforts, we must take the turn within in order to grow, to change, to find that person who is the goal of the journey.

The Persona-Shadow Dialogue

The breakdown of ego domination, the illusion that one knows who one is and is in control, invariably leads to a collision between the persona and the shadow. The persona-shadow dialogue at midlife represents a necessary balancing of the personality between the *Realpolitik* of society and the truth of the individual.

The persona (Latin for "mask") is a more or less conscious adaptation of the ego to the conditions of social life. We develop many personae, roles which are necessary fictions. We are one way with our parents, another with an employer, another with a lover. Although the persona is a necessary interface with the outer world, we tend both to confuse the persona of others with their inner truth and to think that we too are our roles. As suggested earlier, when our roles change we experience a loss of self. The persona feigns individuality but fundamentally, as Jung notes, it "is nothing real: it is a compromise between individual and society."[34] To the degree that we have identified with the persona, our socialized self, so we will suffer anxiety at being pulled away from the outer adaptation to address the reality of the inner. One aspect of the Middle Passage, then, is a radical alteration in our relationship to our persona.

---

[34] *Two Essays on Analytical Psychology,* CW 7, par. 246.

Since much of the first half of life involves the construction and maintenance of the persona, we often neglect our inner reality. Enter the shadow, which represents everything that has been repressed or gone unrecognized.[35] The shadow contains all that is vital yet problematic—anger and sexuality, to be sure, but also joy, spontaneity and untapped creative fires. Freud succinctly observed that the price of civilization is neurosis. The demands of society, beginning with one's family of origin, split off psychic contents and the shadow lengthens. The shadow represents the wounding of one's nature in the interests of collective social values. Accordingly, the confrontation with the shadow and its integration permit a healing of the neurotic split and an agenda for growth. As Jung concluded,

> If it has been believed hitherto that the human shadow was the source of all evil, it can now be ascertained on closer investigation that [it] does not consist only of morally reprehensible tendencies, but also displays a number of good qualities, such as normal instincts, appropriate reactions, realistic insights, creative impulses, etc.[36]

By midlife one has managed to repress large portions of one's personality. Anger, for example, frequently erupts during the Middle Passage because one has been encouraged to suppress it. The Indo-Germanic root *angh,* from which we get anger (and anxiety, angst and angina) means "to constrict." Virtually all socialization represents a constriction of the natural impulses, hence a growing accumulation of anger is to be expected. But where has the energy associated with those natural impulses gone? Often it fuels our blind ambitions and drives us to narcotics to dull its intensity, or leads us to abuse of self or others. If one has been taught that anger is a sin or a moral failing, then one has been split off from one's actual experience of constriction. When acknowledged and channeled, anger can be an enormous stimulus for change. One simply refuses to live inauthentically thereafter. With a life-long investment in the persona, the shadow encounter with anger is troubling, to be sure, but achieving the freedom to feel one's own reality is a necessary step toward healing the inner split.

Other shadow encounters are also painful as one is obliged to acknowledge a continuing catalogue of emotions not normally acceptable to the

---

[35] Repression is an unconscious mechanism by which a thought or impulse is suppressed in order to protect the ego from something that would be too painful to acknowledge.

[36] "The Structure and Dynamics of the Self," *Aion,* CW 9ii, par. 423.

persona world, such as selfishness, dependency, lust and jealousy. Previously, one could deny such qualities and project them onto others—he is vain, she overly ambitious and so on. But, at midlife, the capacity for self-deception is exhausted. In the morning mirror we have seen the enemy—ourselves. While the encounter with one's lesser qualities may be painful, their acknowledgment begins the withdrawal of their projection onto others. Jung felt that the best thing we could do for the world was to withdraw our shadow projections. It takes enormous courage to say that what is wrong in the world is wrong in us, what is wrong in marriage is wrong in us, and so on. But in such humbling moments we begin to improve the world we inhabit, and bring about the conditions for healing of both one's relationships and oneself.

The appointment with oneself also means going back and picking up what was left behind: the *joie de vivre,* the untapped talent, the hopes of the child. If one could see one's own psyche as a mosaic, one would not be able to count, let alone live, all the pieces, but each one affirmed heals and rewards the wounded soul. So the man who wanted to learn to play the piano, the woman who wanted to go to college or drift some summer's afternoon in a rowboat on the bay—each can do what was dreamt and, for whatever reason, left undone. We do not choose our psychic armamentarium, but we can choose to love or neglect its contents. Yet many of us do not feel free to acknowledge our own reality. We lacked sufficient affirmation from the parent, or the example of a parent's embrace of life; we internalized that neglect and the implied interdiction against living our potential. Seizing permission to live one's reality is essential at midlife. The fact that one is mortal, that time is limited, and that no one will deliver us from the burden of responsibility for our lives, serves as a powerful incentive to be more fully oneself.

During the Middle Passage, the insurgence of the shadow is part of a corrective effort made by the Self to bring the personality back into balance. The key to integration of the shadow, the unlived life, is to understand that its demands emanate from the Self, which wishes neither further repression nor unlicensed acting out. The integration of the shadow requires that we live responsibly in society but also more honestly with ourselves. We learn through the deflation of the persona world that we have lived provisionally; the integration of inner truths, joyful or unpleasant, is necessary to bring new life and the restoration of purpose.

Relationship Problems

As suggested earlier, nothing carries more potential for hurt and disappointment at midlife than a long-term intimacy like marriage. Such relationships bear the burden of the inner child. To relationship we bring so much hope, so much need, and so much capacity for disappointment. Anyone who looks back from midlife must shudder at the enormity of such choices as marriage and career, often made decades before, and the unconsciousness out of which they were made. Young people have always fallen in love, promised life-long commitment and made babies. They will continue to do so. But during the Middle Passage many will confront themselves and their partners, putting enormous strain on the relationship. Indeed, there are few midlife marriages, if they have survived, that are not under great strain. Either divorce is the signal event which launches the Middle Passage, or the marriage becomes a prime locus for those tectonic pressures.

To learn more about the role and importance of relationship during the Middle Passage, we need to reflect more deeply on the nature of intimacy. Clearly the person to whom we deliver our soul carries a large weight. In addition, modern culture often assumes that marriage and romantic love are synonymous. For most of history, marriage served as a vehicle for the maintenance and transmission of values, ethnicity, religious tradition and power. Arranged marriages have had a better track record than those predicated on maintaining love, that most elusive of feeling states. Similarly, marriages based on mutual dependence may function well as long as death or destiny does not intervene. (A former colleague, devastated by the experience of the Holocaust, married a woman half his age who took charge of his life to their mutual satisfaction.) Indeed, it would seem from all accounts that marriages based on working needs have a better chance of enduring than those based on romantic expectations and mutual projections. As George Bernard Shaw observed,

> When two people are under the influence of the most violent, most insane, most delusive, and most transient of passions, they are required to swear that they will remain in that excited, abnormal, and exhausting condition continuously until death do them part.[37]

---

[37] Quoted in Gail Sheehy, *Passages: Predictable Crises of Adult Life,* p. 152.

The diagram below shows the transactions which typically occur in heterosexual relationships.

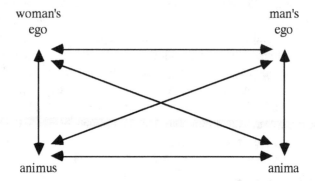

On the conscious level, we have ego relations with others, but we would not contract a romantic alliance based on that ego-relationship. This honor falls to the anima and animus, which are the more or less unconscious contrasexual elements in the psyche.

Very briefly, the anima represents a man's internalized experience of the feminine, influenced initially by his mother and other women, and also colored by something unknown and unique to him. His experience of his anima represents his relationship to his own body, his instincts, his feeling life and his capacity for relationship with others. The woman's animus is her experience of the masculine principle, influenced by father and culture, but mysteriously unique to her also. It embodies her sense of grounding, her capacities, her ability to focus her energies and achieve her desires in the world. However, the fundamental truth of relationship is that one projects all that one does not consciously experience of oneself onto the Other. The diagonal arrows show this projection from anima/animus to ego, and vice versa.[38] Of the many persons of the opposite gender, only a few will attract, those who are good hooks for the projection and can at least temporarily hold it. This diagonal dynamic is behind what is called romantic love.

Romantic love gives one a sense of profound connectedness, new energy, hope and a sense of homecoming. Love at first sight is the most no-

---

[38] For an extended study of this process, see John Sanford, *The Invisible Partners: How the Male and Female in Each of Us Affects Our Relationships.*

table of such projections. The Other could be an ax-murderer, only he or she is able to sustain the projection for the time being. Obviously, behind the projection is only an ordinary human being like us and no doubt projecting a heavy agenda upon us too. But to us the Other is special. "This person is different," we say, or "I never felt like this before." Popular culture feeds the delusion. If all the Top Forty tunes were merged, their lyrics would say something like, "I was miserable until you came into my life and then everything felt brand new and we were on top of the world until you changed and we lost what we had and you moved away and now I am miserable and will never love again until the next time." What varies is the gender of the singer and the presence or not of a guitar.

Living together on a daily basis remorselessly wears away the projections; one is left with the otherness of the Other, who will not and cannot meet the largeness of the projections. So people will conclude at midlife that "You're not the person I married." Actually, they never were. They always were somebody else, a stranger we barely knew then and know only a little better now. Because the anima or animus was projected onto that Other, one literally fell in love with missing parts of oneself. That sense of connectedness and homecoming felt so good and was the occasion of so much hope, that its loss feels catastrophic.[39]

The truth about intimate relationships is that they can never be any better than our relationship with ourselves. How we are related to ourselves determines not only the choice of the Other but the quality of the relationship. In fact, every intimate relationship tacitly reveals who we were when we commenced it. All relationships, therefore, are symptomatic of the state of our inner life, and no relationship can be any better than our relationship to our own unconscious (the vertical axes in the diagram).[40]

Relationship would not be so burdened did we not ask so much of it. But what meaning ought relationship to have if it is not going to deliver on the expectations of the inner child? Meaning comes, Jung noted,

> when people feel they are living the symbolic life, that they are actors in the divine drama. That gives the only meaning to human life;

---

[39] See Aldo Carotenuto, *Eros and Pathos: Shades of Love and Suffering.*

[40] Having spoken thus in public, many have agreed with my logic but felt seriously threatened by the implication that the magical Other is not really out there. One woman came up after my talk and shook her finger in my face and said, "Yes, but I still believe in love." Her angry tone suggested that she had just lost Santa Claus.

everything else is banal and you can dismiss it. A career, producing of children, are all *maya* [illusion] compared to that one thing, that your life is meaningful.[41]

The question then shifts from expecting the magical Other to save us to the role that relationship might play in attaining greater meaning in life.

Clearly the model of intimacy that typifies our culture, and the hopes of the first adulthood, is one of fusion or togetherness—the belief that through union with the Other, the half which I am will be complemented, completed. Together we shall be one; together we shall be whole. Such a natural hope from the person who feels partial and inadequate in the face of the immensity of the world actually serves to impede the development of both. When the abrasion of daily life wears away the hope and its attendant projections, one experiences a loss of meaning, that is, the loss of the meaning as projected onto the Other.

With the perspective of midlife, one is obliged to replace the fusion model because it simply does not work. The model which makes sense for the second half of life, if each person takes on responsibility for his or her psychic well-being, is as follows:

The basin-shaped container suggests the open-ended character of a mature relationship. Each party is primarily in charge of his or her own individuation. Through their relationship they support and encourage each other, but they cannot perform tasks of development, or individuation, for each other. (The importance of individuation will be discussed in chapter five.) This model represents the abandonment of the notion that one will be rescued by the Other. It presupposes that both parties can take on the invitation to individuation and that they serve the partnership by becoming more fully themselves. Having outgrown the fusion model, the mature relationship demands that each partner take personal responsibility, otherwise the marriage will stagnate.

To have a mature relationship one must be able to say, "No one can give me what I most deeply want or need. Only I can. But I can celebrate

---

[41] "The Symbolic Life," *The Symbolic Life,* CW 18, par. 630.

and invest in the relationship for what it does offer." What it usually offers most is companionship, mutual respect and support, and the dialectic of opposites. A young person who uses relationships to prop up a shaky hold on self could not meet the challenge to courage and discipline of a mature relationship. Where one wanted confirmation, one must now accept differences. Where one wanted the simple love of sameness, one must now learn the difficult task of loving otherness.

When one has let go of the projections and the great hidden agenda, then one can be enlarged by the otherness of the partner. One plus one does not equal One, as in the fusion model; it equals three—the two as separate beings whose relationship forms a third which obliges them to stretch beyond their individual limitations. Moreover, by relinquishing projections and placing the emphasis on inner growth, one begins to encounter the immensity of one's own soul. The Other helps us expand the possibilities of the psyche.

Rilke described relationship as the sharing of one's solitude with another.[42] This is certainly close to the truth, for all we have in the end is our solitude. One must acknowledge that the projection will not last, but then again, perhaps it will be replaced by something still richer. Since projections are unconscious, we cannot always be sure we are in a genuine relationship to the Other. But if we have taken that primary responsibility for ourselves, we are far less likely to be projecting the dependencies and unrealistic expectations of the inner child.

Real relationship, then, springs from a conscious desire to share the journey with another, to grow nearer the mystery of life through the bridges of conversation, sexuality and compassion. Nietzsche once observed that marriage was a conversation, a grand dialogue.[43] If one is not prepared to truly engage in dialogue over the long haul, then one is not prepared for long-term intimacy. Many older couples have long since exhausted their conversation because they have ceased to grow as individuals. When the emphasis is on individual growth, then each will have an interesting partner with whom to converse. To block one's own growth, even in the mistaken interest of the other, is to ensure that one's spouse will be living with an angry and depressed person. To be blocked in one's growth by the other is equally not acceptable. The marriage must be opened anew

---

[42] *Letters of Rainer Maria Rilke,* p. 57.
[43] "Human, All Too Human," *The Portable Nietzsche,* p. 59.

or it has lost its reason for being. In the mature marriage, open-ended and dialectical, one may experience the fourth two-way vector of the diagram on page 46, the exchange between two mysteries, the inner contrasexual energies; this is the soul-to-soul encounter.

Love, then, is one way of living the symbolic life to which Jung referred, of encountering the mystery whose name and nature we can never fathom but without whose presence we are trapped in the superficial. By midlife, many marriages are over or in trouble. In the past, individuals who lived through the withdrawal of projections were under too much collective pressure to seek alternatives. There were affairs for some, substance abuse for others, sublimation through work and children for others, and illness, migraines or depression for still others. Positive choices were generally beyond reach. Today there are such choices, and, painful as they may be, they are not as bad as remaining within a structure which does not serve the individuation of the partners. Despite good intentions and much ego volition, the truth will out. It takes courage to examine that structure which has carried one's hopes and one's needs, but courage can heal, restore integrity and bring life after death.

It is a cruel self-deception to believe in the magical Other. Should such a person be found, one can be sure that it is a projection. If after an appropriate lapse of time one is still being taken care of by the Other, then it is very likely that one is stuck in a dependency that the Other feeds or serves, consciously or unconsciously. This is not to diminish the powerful supporting role one's partner can play in our journey, but it is to say that what one flees always is that awesome largeness of personal responsibility for our own lives. I once knew a very competent woman who escorted her husband out the door one morning and installed her husband-to-be the same afternoon. While proficient in her profession, she was not up to the experiment in living with herself and suffering the inner dialogue.

When one has the courage to turn within, one has the opportunity to open to those neglected parts of one's own personality. If one lifts off of the partner the imperative for incarnating life's meaning, then one is called to the activation of one's own potential.

I recently heard a classic gender-role replay of the inner tapes we all receive in early life. Poised at the brink of divorce, a husband and wife blamed each other for what had happened to their lives. The man said he had worked hard to be a success, which meant to advance professionally and support his family. He did this faithfully, but with a growing resentment that he had no life of his own. His anger turned inward, he became depressed, and finally he felt he had to leave the marriage or die. His wife responded that she had played her role as Minister of the Interior and had taken care of him, the home and their children, and had not lived out her professional goals. She too was depressed.

Clearly, both were victims. They had been handed the gender-role tapes and had played them to the best of their ability, as had their respective parents, and grown resentful over the twenty years. Each had also been an accomplice in their unhappiness, but what can we expect of a twenty-some year old other than to play out the script of the first adulthood? They had served the institution of marriage well, but the institution had not served them. Whether they were to stay together or not depended on a mutual commitment to personal growth.

The unwavering truth of the psyche is: change or wither into resentment; grow or die within. Again, the tragedy of marriage at midlife is that often the relationship is so contaminated by resentment that the possibilities for renewal are fatally compromised. Whether good will can be resurrected, and the projection of negativity onto the spouse be withdrawn, is always problematic.

Balancing one's obligations to others and the obligation to oneself is admittedly difficult, but it is essential to try. This issue is not new. Ibsen's *A Doll's House* is surprisingly modern. When Nora walks out on her husband and children she is reminded of her duty to church, husband and children. She replies that she has a duty to herself as well. Her spouse is uncomprehending. Will we be able to patch this up, he asks? Nora replies that she cannot say because, having discovered that she does not know who she is, and that (in effect) she has only been serving the tapes of the first adulthood, she cannot predict who that person will be whom she is determined to discover. When *A Doll's House* was performed a century ago in the capitals of Europe, riots ensued, so great was the implied threat to the institutions of marriage and parenthood. Even now, there are the same obstacles of public opinion, parental models and guilt to confront before walking out the door, or even changing a constricting pattern. Nora walked out of the domestic circle into social ostracism and economic privation, for the law would have forbidden her property, custody or economic rights. But she knew she had to walk or she would die.

The sooner each partner can embrace the necessity of individuation as the *raison d'être* of the relationship, the greater the chance it will last.

There is a natural assumption that somehow time will solve the distress in the head, the hollowness of the stomach. When I ask couples to consider being ten years older with nothing changed, then they are usually clearer that something has to move. When one spouse continues to block change, be assured that he or she is still controlled by anxiety and invested in the projections of the first adulthood. Quite possibly the recalcitrant spouse will forever resist taking on the necessary responsibility; if so, he or she thereby forfeits the right of veto over anyone else's life. No one has the right to block the development of another; that is a spiritual crime.

When partners can recognize their unhappiness and ask each other frankly for support, there is every possibility that the marriage will be renewed. The partner is then neither rescuer nor enemy, only partner. Perhaps the ideal model for couple therapy would be for each person to be in individual therapy, to get a better fix on developmental needs, as well as attending sessions together to deal not only with exhausted patterns of the past but hopes and plans for the future. Thus the marriage could become the container for individuation.

To bring about an attitude of collaboration rather than conflict, I often ask certain questions in the presence of the spouse. For example, "What is it in your history or your behavior which might cause conflict or undermine the relationship?" This startles those who think they have come to someone who will help them validate their case against the other. The question requires them to start looking within and take on a larger responsibility for the care and feeding of the relationship. Another helpful question is, "What have been your dreams for yourself and what fears have blocked you?" Hearing of the spouse's struggles and disappointments, the partner often feels compassion and a desire to support the struggle. The sharing of one's sense of failure, one's fears and hopes, is true intimacy and few couples, however long married, ever achieve it. Sex may be a bridge between them, children as well, but the real cement is to know what it is like to live inside the other's skin.

We can never love our partner's otherness unless we have a good sense of what it is to be that person. Perhaps love is really the capacity to imagine the experience of the Other so vividly that we can affirm that being. True conversation aids this kind of imagining and is the antidote to narcissistic preoccupation. I have heard it questioned whether the concern for personal growth were not itself narcissistic. It is not, as long as one is determined to fulfill one's potential and to grant that same right to the Other.

This requires a double strength: the ability to take responsibility for oneself and the courage to imaginatively validate the reality of the Other. Neither strength is effectively modeled in our culture, so we must find it ourselves. The alternative is precisely the sad state of so many marriages. We blame the spouse because we are unhappy and we secretly suspect we are accomplices. These are sour juices in which to stew a marriage.

Many, such as Carol Gilligan in *In a Different Voice,* have suggested that it is harder for women than for men to affirm their individuation needs because of the enormous claims the relationship makes upon them. The essence of feminine consciousness may be described as diffuse awareness, which means that a woman is very much aware of her surroundings and the claims others make upon her. So, Gilligan reports, her seminar of women agreed with young Stephan Dedaelus, who in James Joyce's autobiographical *Portrait of the Artist as a Young Man* announces, as did Joyce himself, that he is leaving his family, his faith and his nation, for he could no longer serve that which no longer served him. But they identified with Mary McCarthy's dilemma in her *Confessions of a Catholic Girlhood;* when she wanted to make her leap into the unknown she was restrained and paralyzed by duty and guilt. While permission to choose one's own path may be slightly more available to women today than it was to their mothers, most still feel constrained by the claims others place on them. Therefore, a woman may have a greater leap to make than a man toward her right to be herself. Like Nora in *A Doll's House,* she needs to balance the claims of others against her duty to herself. In the end, martyrs make neither good mothers nor good partners. There is always a price for a woman's sainthood; both she and others will pay.

The attachment needs of childhood remain very strong within the adult. We may even say they are natural and normal. But maturity is lacking when the primary measure of one's self-worth and security is invested in the Other. The term "attachment hunger" describes the pattern when the natural needs for the Other are out of hand.[44] What is forgotten, of course, is that one has a ready companion within oneself, at least potentially.

A great problem for many men is that the chest is a numbed zone.[45]

---

[44] Howard M. Halpern, *How to Break Your Addiction to a Person,* pp. 13ff.

[45] The causes of this psychic numbing are explored in such studies as Guy Corneau, *Absent Fathers, Lost Sons;* Robert Bly, *Iron John;* Robert Hopcke, *Men's Dreams, Men's Healing;* and Sam Keen, *Fire in the Belly.*

Conditioned to shun feeling, avoid instinctual wisdom and override his inner truth, the average male is a stranger to himself and others, a slave to money, power and status. In Philip Larkin's haunting lines, they are

> men whose first coronary is coming like Christmas; who drift, loaded helplessly with commitments and obligations and necessary observances, into the darkening avenues of age and incapacity, deserted by everything that once made life sweet.

There are few models in our culture that invite or permit a man to be honest with himself. When asked what he feels, a man will often explain what he thinks, or what the problem "out there" is. Consider the very skillful, tacit message of beer commercials that seem to come with every televised sport. A macho group of merry fellows hoists girders into place, saws logs or drives fork-lifts. (Never do they sit in front of personal computers or hold children.) The whistle blows and it's Miller Time by Bud's early Lite! They stride forth to the nearby watering hole and are allowed to touch each other with comradely familiarity. At the bar they hoist the suds, accompanied by a token blond, suggesting they are not gay and representing the anima who is about to be called forth in joy, or anger, or sentiment. Alcohol, by loosening the defensive strictures against the woman within, promotes what cannot be consciously acknowledged.

How can women expect to have good relationships with men when men do not have a relationship with their own feminine soul? Women cannot be that inner connection; they can only receive and partially carry the man's projection of her. The survival of the ancient Egyptian text, *The World-Weary Man in Search of His Ba* (soul), tells us the problem is not new. What may be new is the growing invitation to men to go within and find what is true for them in the face of the enormous pressures to play out the old roles of warrior and economic animal.

Robert Hopcke, in *Men's Dreams, Men's Healing,* suggests that it takes a man about a year in therapy before he is able to internalize and be present to his actual feelings—a year to reach where women are usually able to begin.[46] I suspect he is right, and how many men are ready to undertake a year's therapy just to reach the starting point? Thankfully, some do, but many are adrift and lost. Victims of the patriarchy, they know only the presence or absence of power as a sign of their manhood.[47] So a man,

---

[46] *Men's Dreams, Men's Healing,* p. 12.

[47] As Eugene Monick points out in *Phallos: Sacred Image of the Masculine*

during the Middle Passage, has to become as a child again, face the fear that power masks, and ask the old questions anew. They are simple questions: "What do I want? What do I feel? What must I do to feel right with myself?" Few modern men allow themselves the luxury of such questions. So they trudge off to work and dream of retiring to play golf on some Elysian Field, hopefully before the heart attack arrives. Unless he can humbly ask these simple questions and allow his heart to speak, he has no chance whatsoever. He is bad company for himself and others.

Many women, similarly, are unempowered, their natural strengths eroded by inner voices of negativity. The negative animus whispers dark nothings in their ears: "You can't do that," he says, with a cold grip on the throat. The animus, which among other things represents a woman's creative capacity, her empowerment to live her life and achieve her own desires, hides under the shadow of her mother's model, her father's encouragement (or discouragement), and the constrictive roles offered by society. Women were traditionally told to find fulfillment through the achievements of their husbands and sons. One of the saddest commentaries I have ever read was from the journal of Mary Benson, a thoroughly Victorian woman who, as the wife of Edward, Archbishop of Canterbury, was defined by the dual institutions of marriage and church. When Edward dies, Mary has that appointment with herself and encounters a

> terrible inner sense that all my life . . . was derived from and in answer to distinct, never ceasing claims. . . . There is nothing within, no power, no love, no desire, no initiative: he had it all and his life entirely dominated mine. Good Lord, give me a personality. . . . The Vision of Personality. . . . How to connect this with finding myself? I feel as if I had led a superficial life so long, not willfully or wrongly exactly. But united as I was with so dominant a personality as Edward . . . combined with the tremendous claims of the position, how was I to find myself? I seem only to have been a service of respondings and no core. But there must be a core.[48]

Reader, look within and tremble. Has Mary's life been yours? As sad as her commentary may be, and as forgivable, given the weight of those sanc-

---

and *Castration and Male Rage: The Phallic Wound,* the patriarchy, with its emphasis on power, hierarchical thinking and aggression, is the refuge of those who do not feel grounded in a deep masculine sensibility. Wounded thus, they wound both women and other men.

[48] Katherine Moore, *Victorian Wives,* pp. 89-90.

tioned powers, we must hold her responsible in the end. Personality is not given by the Lord; it is attained in the daily struggle against the demons of doubt and disapproval whose progeny are depression and desuetude.

Rather than suffer definition by gender role, modern women struggle valiantly to balance career and family. Little is left over for the dreams of the past. Often a woman is left at midlife both by children, who are rightly engaged in their own lives, and by husband, captured by work or the new woman onto whom his anima projection has fallen. One might say she has a right to feel betrayed and abandoned, but then again, perhaps if she had consciously foreseen and prepared for such events, she might welcome her new-found freedom.

I know a father who said to his daughter as she left for college, "Gⁱ the averages on divorce, and the fact that men die earlier, you have a eighty per cent chance of living by yourself, with or without children to support, and without the finances to do it. Therefore, you had better have a profession of your own and enough self-esteem that your sense of worth does not depend on the man in your life." These were not words of optimism, not an admonition to get married for security, not the encouragement to dependency her mother might have received from her mother. They were not words he enjoyed saying. Their only merit was their truth.

When a woman feels abandoned at midlife, her inner child rises quickly to the surface. This is a traumatic experience. If she seeks therapy, the first year is spent venting grief and anger, overcoming disbelief and accepting the abrogation of that tacit contract we thought we had with the universe. During the second year she gathers her energies for a new life. If she has not the education or job skills necessary for economic survival, she does what she can to acquire them. She may have every reason, from a collective point of view, to feel that others took advantage of her. In therapy she may acknowledge her unconscious collusion.

For many women presently in the Middle Passage, now is the time to keep the appointment with themselves, invited but missed years ago. When the mantle of nurturer to all drops away, the woman is obliged to ask anew who she is and what she wants to do with her life. She cannot resolve such matters until she becomes more conscious of the various inner forces which block her, the complexes acquired from mother and father and from Western culture.[49] The negative energy of the animus erodes

---

[49] Among the excellent studies of the balancing act between animus devel-

will, confidence and self-belief. The animus as positive energy represents empowerment, the capacity to engage in and fight for what one wants, and the assertion of the life force. Positive animus energy is seldom given; it is achieved. Finding the courage to risk a new definition of herself, one which values relationship but is not limited or defined by it, is the task of the midlife woman.

Midlife Affairs

Occasionally, the forces within rise with a vengeance and overwhelm the person. The incidence of extramarital affairs reportedly hovers around fifty per cent, men only slightly ahead of women. I imagine few of them woke in the morning and said, "I think I will screw my life up today, risk hurting my spouse and my children, risk losing all I have fought to attain." But it happens.

Whatever merits the third party may have in reality, she or he will certainly be the bearer of projections. Just as marriage is the prime bearer of the needs of the inner child, so the affair is the prime bearer of the renewed anima-animus projection when the marital partner has proved to be merely human. As I write, a certain well-known actress has announced her eighth, or is it ninth, marriage. I wish her well, but I know at this late age she is still projecting. Her present choice is a hunk some twenty years her junior. As I write, I am seeing a man, forty-eight, in love with a twenty-one-year-old girl. I see his raft heading over the Niagara but nothing I might say can stop him. I have not met her, of course. I do not know how nagging his wife is, of course. I cannot fathom how much he feels renewed, of course. The power of the unconscious requires more respect than logic, tradition and the Constitution of the United States.

Freud used to require that his patient make no major decisions, marriage, divorce, career, while in analysis. Perhaps this is sound theoretically, but life flows onward, emotions occur, decisions are demanded and one must continue to function in the real world. No matter that the projection will dissolve; no matter that one will be stuck with oneself in any case; life flows onward and choices are made. In working with couples I

---

opment and grounded femininity are Linda Leonard's *The Wounded Woman,* which deals with the father-daughter impact; Kathie Carlson's *In Her Image: The Unhealed Daughter's Search For Her Mother,* which treats the mother-daughter relationship; and Marion Woodman's *Addiction to Perfection, The Pregnant Virgin,* and *The Ravaged Bridegroom.*

am always relieved if there is no third party, for then I know that the partners have a chance to work through their marriage honestly. If it has failed, then let us acknowledge that directly, but let us not shunt things off onto the side track, the projections which affairs incarnate. When people are in active affairs, I urge them to suspend contact as much as possible in order to look realistically at their marriage. Sometimes this strategy works, and a husband or wife is able to address the marriage unencumbered. But most of the time I am spitting into the wind. Individuals possessed by contents of the unconscious are unable to be realistic.

The power of the affair at midlife really lies in the magnetic pull back to the full flush of first adulthood. Just as often as I have heard women lament that their husbands became involved with a sweet young thing, so I have seen women get involved with older men. What does that tell us? It suggests that men with inadequate anima development are attracted to women at a similar level. It also suggests that women, with inadequate animus development, are attracted to the worldly power of an older man. Given the paucity of rites of passage for men and women, it is no wonder that so many of us are seeking mentoring, even from lovers. Men go to younger women, reflecting their immature anima; women gravitate toward men with status or age, in compensation for their own insufficient animus development. No wonder the affair has so much numinosity. It really embraces one's lost soulfulness. Yet affairs often bring even more sadness and loss. A wise therapist, Mae Rohm, once said, "The screwing you get is not worth the screwing you get."[50] But try telling that to a person in an affair. Try telling it to a person being hurt by a spouse's affair.

Having suggested that the model of marriage for the first adulthood is one of fusion, now we can see how complicated relationships can be. It is astonishing that any relationship works at all. Given the immensity of unconscious forces, the projections, the parental complexes, etc., how can anyone ever be honestly related to another? At first we may be inclined to say, look at history, people have functioned rather well. Then we are forced to admit, of history and our own experience, no, they have not. It has been a grand, confusing, hurtful mess. I am inclined to see the person not as a half seeking its other half—the fusion model—but as a polyhedron, a sphere of many facets. There is no way in the world, even with Miss Perfect or Mr. Wonderful, that one may line up all of the planes of two poly-

---

[50] Personal communication.

hedrons. At best a few. Is this an argument for affairs?—certainly! But it is a bad argument. I have known a few so-called open marriages, some managed by highly conscious individuals. All failed in the end, in part because, however rational the agreement, there are such things as feelings. Even in the most rational of contracts there is jealousy, longing and the need to know where one stands. So, if the metaphor of the polyhedron makes any sense, we can only match up a few of those facets with one person. It represents an argument for multiple friendships, for sure, but this is certainly possible without crossing the sexual frontier.

The ability to acknowledge the polyhedronal image of personality, which frees the individual though it may threaten the spouse, may also be the ability to choose development. To a person in the first adulthood, for whom the Other is the prime source of support, the polyhedronal model is a threat. Naturally, given the inner child with all its needs, the solution is outer—"out there is the Other who will heal and restore me." But when one suffers the excitation and exhaustion, and ultimately, the depression, of the affair, then one may be ready to ask what it has all meant. When so many have extramarital affairs, one must say that such a pattern has great meaning. I suggest that the meaning is both diffuse, emotionally, and very specific, conceptually.

The meaning of the midlife affair is the imperative to go back and pick up what was left behind in one's development. Since what was undeveloped agitates from below consciousness, it is still unknown. What remains unconscious is projected upon another who, in the mysterious scanning of the unconscious, lines up with the undeveloped areas. What is sought is completion, wholeness. What is surprising about such a search for wholeness? But, try explaining all this to a person in love! Affairs will persist because the vastness of the unknown persists. Yes, the Other in the affair may in fact prove to be a wonderful person, the true soul-mate. If he or she did not have some of that, the projection would not have occurred in the first place. If the new liaison survives, then one *may* have integrated something missing in the first adulthood. Or one has been very lucky. Or one is in for a very large disappointment.

Perhaps the hardest task of all is learning to accept and affirm one's separateness in the context of relationship. The theme which recurs throughout this discussion is the necessity of taking responsibility for one's own well-being while still being responsive to others. Attachment needs persist, for sure, even as one gains greater independence. Just as the affair promises to connect one with those needs unaddressed by the marriage, so the marriage is burdened by the resentment and anger which accrues from needs unmet. The easiest thing in the world is to blame another. Why does the person having the affair justify it by saying, "I can talk to you but I can't to my spouse"?

In reality one can probably talk more to one's spouse than to a comparative stranger. It is rather that the marital conversation has become so encrusted with inhibition, repetition and disappointment that one has given up the hope of truly meeting the Other in the ordinariness of one's spouse. Moreover, the mysterious Other in the affair is undoubtedly attracting and embodying the projection of the undeveloped parts of one's polyhedronal self. The marriage hardly has a chance when ranged against the numinosity of the encounter with the reflections of one's own soul. It is, therefore, a work of enormous will on the part of the participants to pull back from the affair and bring those missing parts, those unattempted conversations, back to the original partnership.

How often have I seen true sharing of feelings, aspirations and previous wounds only in therapy or in divorce court. It is not so much that the marriage has failed; it has never really been tried. If marriage is, as Nietzsche suggested, a grand conversation, most marriages do not meet the test. True sharing of what it is like to live within one's own skin and what it is like for the Other seldom occurs. People can live together, make babies and support a family structure, yet never really apprehend the mystery of their partner. The sadness of such an outcome is at times overwhelming.

It is eminently possible for a marriage to enter the whirlpool of the Middle Passage, to deconstruct and be reconstituted if, and this is a big if, the two are willing to become separate persons again and dialogue with each other about that separateness. One must acknowledge the paradox that for marriage to be unified there must first be greater separateness. Marital therapy may address the resolution of conflict, the identification and correction of poor strategies and the establishment of an agenda for growth. This is clearly important and can help to improve the experience of marriage, but genuine renewal does not occur unless the persons involved are changed. Each person must become more fully an individual before there can be a transformation of the relationship. A marriage can only be as good as, or at the level of, the two persons in it.

The transformation of marriage at midlife, then, involves three necessary steps:

1) The partners must assume responsibility for their own psychological well-being.

2) They must commit to sharing the world of their own experience without reproaching the Other for past wounds or future expectations. Similarly, they are to endeavor to hear, without feeling defensive, the experience of the Other.

3) They must commit to sustaining such a dialogue over time.

These three steps ask a great deal. But the alternative is that marriages limp along or dissolve. Radical conversation is what a long-term commitment is about. With or without a wedding ceremony, true marriage is seldom achieved without radical conversation. Only radical conversation, the full sharing of what it is like to be me while hearing what it is really like to be you, can fulfill the promise of an intimate relationship. One can only engage in radical conversation if one has taken responsibility for oneself, has some self-awareness, and has the tensile strength to withstand a genuine encounter with the truly Other.

Loving the otherness of the partner is a transcendent event, for one enters the true mystery of relationship in which one is taken to the third place—not you plus me, but we who are more than ourselves with each other.

From Child to Parent to Child

Earlier I noted that one of the characteristics of the Middle Passage is an altered relationship to one's parents. We not only deal with parents in a new context of empowerment, we also watch their decline; but even more important we learn to differentiate ourselves. Perhaps no task is more important at midlife than the separation from parental complexes, for the simple reason that those powerful influences supported the false self discussed earlier, the provisional identity acquired during the first adulthood. Until we can recognize the reactive rather than generative character of the first adulthood, we are literally not ourselves.

However troubled or benign one's childhood experience, the power of the world was "out there," in the big people. As a child I was deeply impressed when my father pulled a fishhook from his hand without wincing or crying. I concluded either that adults felt less pain, or, more likely, that he knew how to handle his pain. I hoped he would teach me that wonderful skill, for I knew how much I feared pain. Similarly, without having a clue as to what puberty was, I noticed that beyond eighth grade the kids sud-

denly had big bodies, went to a place called high school and had a knowledge of the world I lacked. How this mysterious transformation occurred I
did not know, but I guessed that "they" took the young people aside and
taught them how to be big people. I had stumbled on the need for those
rites of passage into adulthood which assisted our ancestors but are absent
in our era. The reader may share my disappointment in arriving at that
happy transit into the world of the big people without illumination, dis-
covering rather acne, sexual confusion and a growing awareness that "they"
did not know anything magical either.

The first adulthood is informed, then, not by true knowledge of the inner and outer worlds, but by confusion and dependence on the instructions
and models of parents and institutions. As David Wagoner writes in "The
Hero with One Face":

> I chose what I was told to choose:
> They told me gently who I was. . . .
> I wait, and wonder what to learn:
> O here, twice blind at being born.[51]

There are several aspects of the parent complex one must work through
at midlife. At the most visceral level, the experience of the parent was a
primal message about life itself, how supportive or hurtful it was, and
how warm or cold our welcome. How well, or poorly, did a parental figure
mediate the child's natural anxiety? Therein lies the formation of the core
angst which underlies all our attitudes and behaviors.

Secondly, the parent-child experience constituted the primary encounter
with power and with authority. The imperative to find one's own authority
is essential in midlife; otherwise the second half remains dominated by the
vagaries of childhood. By what authority, that is, normative set of values,
do we live? Who says so? Most adults spend a lot of time "checking in."
Thus, one must try to catch, render conscious, all the conversations which
go on within. How many times does one consult or ask permission from
the invisible presences in the head? The inner dialogue is more ingrained,
more insidious, than one might ever imagine. Who is the "me" who is
"checking in?" Who are "they?" Chances are those inner authorities are
mother or father or their surrogates.

The reflexive character of this "checking in" is astonishing. It can only
be combatted by noting when one feels distressed by a decision or conflict.

---

[51] *A Place To Stand,* p. 23.

When one is able to stop and ask, simply, "Who am I at this moment? What do I feel, what do I want?"—then one is not in the reflexive pattern, but in the present. The insidious nature of "checking in" is that one is living in the past. I knew a man who, whenever he was about to confide something personal or say something about someone else, would look over his shoulder, even in the privacy of the analytic session. He called this "the German glance." He had grown up during the Nazi era and like his contemporaries had learned to look over his shoulder whenever speaking anything private or possibly against an authority. Though fifty years and four thousand miles away from that place of adolescence, his body and his psyche recalled, "checked in." So we all reflexively check in with the authorities of our past.

Religious dictates play such a role for many people, and they are infantilized by the lack of freedom to express their feelings without guilt. I have seen perhaps more damage than good done to people by authoritarian and unconscious clergy. Guilt and the threat of exclusion from the community serve as powerful deterrents to the development of the individual. (It was no accident that the ancients considered exile the worst punishment which could be visited upon a person. The orthodox Jew chants the Kaddish, the prayer for the dead, for the one who goes outside the community; the Amish "shun" those who march to a different drummer.) Exile from the group is the great threat of authority. No child can withstand exclusion from parental approval and protection, and so it learns reflexively to curb natural impulses. The name for that defense against the angst of exclusion is guilt. So great is the threat of the loss of home, so terrifying the loss of the parent, that we all, to some degree, continue to check in. The "German glance" is in us all whether our body moves or not.

Without the ability to live in the present, to live as a self-defining adult, one remains a prisoner of the past, estranged from one's own nature and adulthood. To awaken to that inauthenticity is at first demoralizing but ultimately liberating. How humbling it is to recognize the inner dependency on outer authority projected onto spouse, boss, church or state. How frightening it often seems, even today, to choose one's own path. As one analysand said recently, "I was told that to consider myself was to be selfish. Even today I feel guilty when I refer to myself or use the word *self.*"

The obverse side of dealing with the parent complexes and the struggle for personal authority is how much of one's identity is invested in children. Many parents project their unlived life onto their child. Already mentioned as classic examples are the Stage-Door Mother and Little-League Father. Sylvia Plath's mother even attempted to manage her daughter's career after the poet's suicide. A child often receives mixed messages from such a parent. "Be successful and you will make me happy, but don't be so successful that you leave me behind." Thus the child experiences the love of the parent as conditional. The parent's identification is usually strongest with the same-sex child although often a parent will unconsciously live out the anima or animus through the other sex child. Many boys have had to carry their mother's ambitions; many girls have had to carry their father's anima, as Gail Godwin details in *Father Melancholy's Daughter.* The extremity of such projection is illustrated in sexual abuse where the parent's anima or animus is functioning at a childish level.

It can seem a very fine line between lovingly protecting and nurturing a child, or living through the child inappropriately. Again, as Jung pointed out, the greatest burden on the child is the unlived life of the parent. When the parent's own life has been blocked by anxiety, for example, the child will find it hard to overcome barriers and may even get stuck in an unconscious loyalty to the parent's level of development. But a parent who is living his or her life is not unconsciously jealous, not projecting expectations and limitations onto the child. The more individuated the parent, the freer the child can be. E.E. Cummings describes one such relationship:

> —i say though hate were why men breathe—
> because my father lived his soul
> love is the whole and more than all.[52]

Lincoln said, "As I would not be a slave, so I would not be a master."[53] So the same freedom to become ourselves we wished our parents to bestow upon us, we must grant to our own children. We have had to struggle to be ourselves and we often wish our parents had recognized that we were meant for different paths from the outset. So we must free our children. It has been observed that the friction between adolescents and parents is nature's way of breaking the bond of mutual dependency. While most parents are happy when their children go off to college, find work or get married, many still feel a partial loss of selfhood, that part which has been identified with the child. I know several parents who call their adult

---

[52] "My Father Moved Through Dooms of Love," in *Poems 1923-1954,* p. 375.
[53] *The Lincoln Treasury,* p. 292.

children every day, sometimes several times a day. This is a tacit message of mutual dependency and no favor to the child. It retards that person from the necessity of taking hold of the first adulthood.

Many parents are disappointed in their children because they did not go to the right college or marry the right person, or perhaps because they don't espouse the right value system. Their disappointment is in direct proportion to seeing the child as an extension of themselves and not as a different being with a unique path of its own. If we truly love our children, the single best thing we can do for them is to individuate as much as possible ourselves, for this frees them to do the same.

Contrary to popular assumptions, an analyst does not have a plan for how an analysand ought to individuate. The analyst seeks to promote the inner dialogue, trusting that the voice of the Self will manifest and hoping that the analysand will come to trust his or her inner truth. This approach treats the patient as worthy of respect and incarnating a mysterious call, the unfolding of which is the purpose of life. And just so should we treat our children—worthy of being different, having no obligation to us whatsoever. They are not here to take care of us; *we* are here to take care of us. As in marriage, the task is to love the otherness of the Other. Feeling guilty for not having been the perfect parent, or seeking to protect our children from the trials of life, does not serve them well. The desire to control, to have them live out our incomplete lives, to replicate our value system, is not love; it is narcissism and it impedes their journey. It is difficult enough to individuate. Why should they carry our needs as well? Letting go of children during our Middle Passage—if we haven't already— is not only helpful to them but necessary for us, since it releases energy for our own further development.

Another aspect of the parent complex which must often be confronted at midlife is how the experience of our parents' relationship affected our capacity for intimacy. The model of intimacy to which the child is exposed is formative. The adolescent is generally convinced that he or she will choose a different partner from the one chosen by the parent, adopt a different style of relating and avoid the pitfalls of the parental marriage. Guess again! As long as the parent complexes are active, one will choose the same kind of person or overcompensate in the opposite direction. This only becomes apparent over time. Thus it is a shock to realize at midlife that one is more like one's parent than one thought and that one's relationship follows some familiar patterns. Accordingly, changing oneself at midlife may necessitate a hard look at one's intimate relationship as well. Inner change often makes necessary collateral change in the relationship, whether the partner is equally inclined or not. Sadly, sometimes the insinuation of the parent complex has been so profound as to have irretrievably contaminated the marriage. (The spill-over to marriage from the parental complexes is akin to what the military, describing civilian casualties, calls "collateral damage.")

Recall Jung's concept of the complex. It represents an emotionally charged cluster of energy within the psyche which is partially split off from the ego and therefore can operate autonomously. It is essentially an emotional reflex whose strength depends upon the power or duration of its genesis. Some complexes are positive, though we tend to focus on those which have a negative, interruptive influence in life. Obviously the mother and father complexes will be powerful, given their enormous role in early life. Perhaps it would be useful to dramatically illustrate the role of the positive and negative parental complexes through the work of a poet.

Many modern poets have abandoned the notion carried by their literary ancestors that they can address the Zeitgeist as a whole. Rather, they tend to reflect on their personal lives, seeking some sense there, and hoping through the power of the word to touch the lives of others. Such poetry, often called "confessional," is both intimately personal and universal, in that we share the same human condition. Let us look at three poems by the contemporary American poet, Stephen Dunn, for examples. The first is called "The Routine Things Around the House."

> When mother died
> I thought: now I'll have a death poem.
> That was unforgivable
>
> yet I've since forgiven myself
> as sons are able to do so
> who've been loved by their mothers.
>
> I stared into the coffin
> knowing how long she'd live,
> how many lifetimes there are
>
> in the sweet revisions of memory.
> It's hard to know exactly
> how we ease ourselves back from sadness,
>
> but I remembered when I was twelve,
> 1951, before the world

unbuttoned its blouse.

I had asked my mother (I was trembling)
if I could see her breasts
and she took me into her room

without embarrassment or coyness
and I stared at them,
afraid to ask for more.

Now, years later, someone tells me
Cancers who've never had mother love
are doomed and I, a Cancer,

feel blessed again. What luck
to have had a mother
who showed me her breasts

when girls my age were developing
their separate countries,
what luck

she didn't doom me
with too much or too little.
Had I asked to touch,

perhaps to suck them,
what would she have done?
Mother, dead woman

who I think permits me
to love women easily,
this poem

is dedicated to where
we stopped, to the incompleteness
that was sufficient

and to how you buttoned up,
began doing the routine things
around the house.[54]

   Here Dunn explicitly works with the mother complex, as he not only remembers the past but is able to observe its consequences beneath his present. To become conscious of such experiences and their silent influence is a necessary task of the Middle Passage.

---

[54] *Not Dancing,* pp. 39-40.

In this poem one can see the effect of a positive mother radiating in a number of directions. Most of all, having felt his mother's love, the poet is able to accept, even forgive, himself. We cannot love ourselves unless we have felt affirmed by the parent. Secondly, Dunn realizes that his first experience of the feminine was so positively charged that he could transfer this trust and love to other women. Obviously, he treads dangerous ground here, even as he ventured into the forbidden as a child. Visiting the Other is like visiting a foreign planet. If one's initial visit was supported and supportive, subsequent visits may similarly be so. The third radiant from the mother—the first two being the experience of being loved and the encounter with the mystery of the Other—is the imputation of wisdom to her. She knew, for instance, how much to honor the child's need to know, without destroying either mystery or privacy. Note too that the recalled encounter is placed in the context of the ordinary, highlighting its impact as nontraumatic and psychologically positive.

In addition to the maintenance of the security of the child, the parent's deepest role is archetypal. That is, whatever the child experiences in the parent both serves as model for the child and activates similar capacities within the child itself.

Naturally, the parent is often the child of incomplete parents and can only model and transmit his or her own experience. Thus the legacy of wounded, partial souls is passed from generation to generation. The two greatest needs of the child are for nurturance and empowerment. Nurturance implies that the world will serve and meet us half way, support and feed us, physically and emotionally. Empowerment implies that we possess the wherewithal to meet life's challenges and to fight for what we desire. While either parent or both may nurture and encourage empowerment, nurturing is archetypally associated with the feminine principle and empowerment with the masculine.

In a long, many-part poem titled "Legacy," Dunn traces the evolution of his father's role in the family mythos. The first poem within a poem is titled "The Photograph" and represents the child's encounter with the archetype of implied empowerment.

> My father is in Captain Starns,
> a restaurant in Atlantic City.
> It's 1950,
> I'm there too, eleven years old.
> He sold more Frigidaires

than anyone. That's why we're there,
everything free.
It's before the house started
to whisper, before testimony
was called for and lives got ruined.

My father is smiling. I'm smiling.
There's a bowl of shrimp
in front of us.
We have identical shirts on,
short sleeve with little sailboats.
It's before a difference set in

between corniness and happiness.
Soon I'll get up
and my brother will sit next to him.
Mother will click the shutter.
We believe in fairness,

we still believe America
is a prayer, an anthem.
Though his hair is receding
my father's face says nothing
can stop him.[55]

One senses the poet's nostalgia (from the Greek meaning "pain for home") in these lines. The camera has caught a moment, a truth for that moment, a truth which would not be alone among truths, but a truth nonetheless. How is the world to be measured? For T. S. Eliot, "we have measured out our lives in coffee spoons . . . . our only monument, concrete highways and a thousand lost golf balls."[56] For this dad, this child, more Frigidaires than someone's else's dad. It is now a lost childhood, a lost America of simple pieties, but "my father's face says nothing / can stop him." One senses the transmittal of this mystery from father to child even as the mother unveiled another mystery to free the future man.

How differently the child walks into the first adulthood who has not witnessed such mysteries. When the models of the parent are caution, fear, prejudice, codependency, narcissism and powerlessness, the first adulthood is contaminated by their domination or desperate over-compensation for them. Differentiating one's own knowing from the messages of the parent

---

55 Ibid., p. 41.
56 *The Complete Poems and Plays,* p. 5.

is the necessary prelude to the second half of life.

Another poem by Dunn illustrates the task of sorting through crucial questions. "In what ways am I like my mother?" "In what ways different?" "How am I like my father?" "How different?" "Who had the greater impact on me?" "Where was the other one while this was happening?" "How is mine a separate journey in a different time?" Necessary questions. Answers are not always forthcoming, for what stirs us is often unconscious, and we can only begin to discern patterns through repetition or therapy or sudden moments of insight. In "Regardless," written a decade after the previous two, Dunn begins this process.

> Once, my father took me to the Rockaways
>   during a hurricane
> to see how the ocean was behaving,
>
> which made my mother furious, whose love
>   was correct, protective.
> We saw a wooden jetty crumble. We saw water
>
> rise to the boardwalk, felt the wildness
>   of its spray.
> That night: silence at dinner, a storm
>
> born of cooler, more familiar air.
>   My father
> always rode his delightful errors
>
> into trouble. Mother waited for them, alertly,
>   the way the oppressed
> wait for their historical moment.
>
> Weekdays, after six, I'd point my bicycle
>   toward the Fleet Street Inn
> to fetch him for dinner. All his friends
>
> were there, high-spirited lonelies, Irish,
>   full of laughter.
> It was a shame that he was there, a shame
>
> to urge him home. Who was I then but a boy
>   who had learned to love
> the wind, the wind that would go its own way,
>
> regardless. I must have thought damage
>   is just what happens.[57]

---

[57] *Landscape at the End of the Century,* pp. 33-34..

Again we see the parent mediating the mysteries for the child, the storm-swept, wind-frothed sea—father as psychopomp, soul-guide to such wonders. Mother's protective sense, correct but confining—also a form of love, both needed by the child. Two forms of eros, then, colliding at the dinner table, the child in between. The metonymy of the hurricane intimates other, darker storms. Thus, the child between mother and father, a shame to call him home, a shame to be the emissary. Shame is what the child will internalize, the memory of being caught between them, loving both, needing both, needing to follow the currents of his own inner wind, regardless. Years later, the stuff that just happens is discerned as damage. What damage, we ask? What effects? How is that carried today, affecting you and others? Other questions for other poems.

As long as it remains unconscious, one will continue to carry the sadness or the anger or the unlived life of the parent. Shame also, for shame means that one feels implicated in the wounds of others. In the end we can only judge others by the quality of their heart, which is not to say they have not done damage to themselves and others in the meantime. In these three poems by Stephen Dunn we see the positive and negative parental complexes at work. Again, the complex is inevitable for history is inevitable. What is not conscious from our past will infiltrate our present and determine our future. The degree to which we feel nurtured directly affects our ability to nurture others. The degree to which we feel empowered directly affects our ability to lead our own lives. The degree to which we can risk relationship, or even to imagine it as supportive rather than hurtful, is a direct function of our level of conscious dialogue with the parent complexes.

Many of us had wounded parents who could not meet our archetypal needs for nurturance or empowerment. It is essential to examine this personal history during the Middle Passage. I have heard it said that psychotherapy is all about blaming parents for one's miseries. Quite the contrary, the more sensitive we are to the fragility of the human psyche, the more likely are we to forgive parents for being woundable and wounding. The major crime is to remain unconscious, a crime we can ill afford. Wheresoever we find wounds, deficits in our history, there we are obliged to parent ourselves.

Naturally it is much, much harder to achieve what has not been activated in us archetypally. Nothing can be accomplished without enormous risk, for one must venture into a fear-fringed Terra Incognita. If I have experienced betrayal by a parent, I will find it all the more difficult to trust others and hence to risk relationship. I may fear the opposite sex. I may undermine my relations with them, choosing wrongly from the beginning. If I have not had my worth affirmed I will fear failure, avoid success and program myself to a repetitive cycle of evading the tasks of life. Even if I feel no floor beneath me, I still must take step after step, laying down a strip of accomplishment each time until I have built my own floor.

Nothing will be achieved without discerning the origin of those primary messages, their derivation from someone's else's life. Our task is to live more fully, if not with manifest support from the early years, then somehow without it. Jung once observed that we cannot grow up until we can see our parents as other adults, special to our biography certainly, wounded perhaps, but most of all simply other people who did or did not take on the largeness of their own journey. We have our journey, for sure, and that is large enough to take us beyond our personal history toward our full potential.

The World of Work: Job Versus Vocation

By midlife no one needs to be reminded of economic reality. By midlife one has surely learned the truth of the cliché that money will not buy happiness even as we worry about impoverished retirement. But money, as with other projections of the first adulthood, may come to be seen as only pieces of paper and metal which are useful but not important in any ultimate sense. So, each of us has an economic task and an economic wounding. For many women who have nurtured their families, economic freedom constitutes an empowerment denied to them. For many men at midlife, freighted with orthodontic bills and college tuitions, economics constitutes a strait jacket, a never-ending constraint.

To meet these realities most of us will have to work all our lives. For some, work is emotionally sustaining, while for others the dream of retirement beckons like an oasis in the desert. Work may be a necessary component of health, as Freud believed, but what kind of work? There is a huge difference between a job and a vocation. A job is what we hold to earn money to meet economic demands. A vocation (from Latin *vocatus,* calling) is what we are called to do with our life's energy. It is a requisite part of our individuation to feel that we are productive, and not responding to one's calling can damage the soul.

We do not really choose a vocation; rather it chooses us. Our only choice is how we respond. One's vocation may have nothing to do with earning money. One may be called to nurture others. One may be called to be an artist in a time which does not reward art, but we are sustained by saying yes despite neglect, even rejection. Kazantzakis's novel *The Last Temptation of Christ* wrestles with this dilemma. Jesus of Nazareth merely wishes to be like his father, a carpenter who make crosses for the Roman authorities. He wants to marry Mary Magdalene, live in the suburbs, drive a sports version of the camel, and have 2.2 children. The voice within, the *vocatus,* calls him to a different place. His last temptation, experiencing loneliness and abandonment by his father, is to renounce his calling and become an ordinary person. When he imagines his life that way he realizes he would have betrayed himself by betraying his individuation. In saying yes to his *vocatus* Jesus becomes the Christ. So Jung said that the proper *imitatio Christi* was not to live like the Nazarene of old, but to live one's individuation, one's vocation, as fully as Jesus lived the Christ.[58] (This is what St. Paul meant when he said, "Not Christ, but Christ within me.")[59]

Our vocation is seldom a straight path, but a series of unfolding tackings and turnings. A newspaper recently reported that in any given year nearly forty per cent of Americans change their careers; not jobs, careers. This mobility and transition is in part the result of shifting economic opportunities, for sure, but many are changing their lives. We live longer today; there is nothing to prevent a person from having several careers, each activating another facet of the polyhedronal self.

Economic necessity cannot be ignored, of course, but consider the choices. One can spend one's life in economic servitude, or one can say, "This is how I earn my living, a necessary trade-off with the creditors, and that is where my soul is replenished." I knew a man, for example, with a masters degree in philosophy who worked from three until eight a.m. every day delivering newspapers. It was a mindless job to pay the bills, but the rest of the day he was a free man. He found a balance between work and vocation and was served by both.

Some are able to unite their work and their vocation, though they may have to pay an enormous price to achieve this. Ironically, sometimes a

---

[58] "Commentary on 'The Secret of the Golden Flower,'" *Alchemical Studies,* CW 13, par. 81.
[59] Galatians 2: 20.

strong vocation requires even the sacrifice of ego desires. But for vocation one does not ask; one is asked. And a considerable part of the meaning of one's life comes from saying yes when asked. The ego does not run life; it knows very little. It is the mystery of the Self that awesomely asks us to become whole, and how we decide to spend our energy plays a significant role in our journey.

When we recognize and withdraw the projections that money and power represent, then we are obliged to ask in radical form: "What am I called to do?" This question must be asked periodically, and we must listen humbly to the answer. We may, in our individuation process, be called to incarnate many kinds of energy. Just when we have achieved a measure of stability, we may be undermined from below and called to a new direction. Whatever our social burden, whatever our economic constraint, we must keep asking anew, "What am I called to do?" Then, with planning, the paying of dues and sufficient courage, we must find a way to do it. The sacrifice of the ego, with its need for creature comforts and security, is painful, but not half so much as looking back on our lives and regretting that we failed to answer the call. The *vocatus* is to become ourselves as fully as we are able; the task is to find out how. We are judged not only by the goodness of our heart, but also by the fullness of our courage. Relinquishing security we have struggled to obtain may be frightening, but not so much as denying that larger person we are called to be. The soul has its needs, which are not served well by paycheck and perks.

Emergence of the Inferior Function

The complexity of the modern world has generated a world of specialists to meet its needs. So, from grade school on we are grouped according to functions and aptitudes and led into increased specialization. The further we go professionally, the more we risk damage to the personality and blunting of the soul. The importance of the liberal arts has been eroded under the weight of commercial and professional training. So we become constrained by narrowed definitions of academic preparation. Jung's simplest definition of neurosis was "disunity with oneself," a one-sidedness of the personality.[60] That definition would include us all, especially because of the reactive character of the acquired personality discussed earlier, but also because

---

[60] "Psychological Factors in Human Behaviour," *The Structure and Dynamics of the Psyche,* CW 8, par. 255.

of the nature of the education process in Western society. The more trained we are, the more narrow we become as personalities.

In 1921 Jung published a volume describing eight personality typologies, representing the different ways in which we might process reality.[61] His terms *introversion* and *extraversion* have entered our common language. The four functions, *thinking, feeling, sensation* and *intuition* are possessed by all but in differing proportions. The dominant function is the one we most reflexively turn to in order to orient ourselves to reality. Our typology seems to have a genetic base though we are certainly influenced by those around us. The attitude of introversion or extraversion describes whether we tend to process reality as something within or something "out there." Accordingly, an extraverted sensation type will likely be drawn to the outer world and become an engineer, for example, or a chef. An introverted thinking type might become an academic but would be a disaster at selling used cars.

Our dominant functions usually emerge early, and we all tend to ride those dominant orientations as much as we can. Moreover, as suggested above, we are quickly categorized according to what we are good at and further narrowed into our specialties. The more trained we are and the more successful we are with that training, the more narrow will be our vision and our personality. Society rewards us for this and we collude because it is easier to go with our dominant orientation than to struggle with that which is awkward or perhaps less rewarding.[62]

The idea of the dominant function does not imply better, merely more developed and more utilized. The inferior function refers to the mode of reality processing to which one turns least and with which one feels least comfortable. So, a thinking type is not without feelings, but examining what something means, how to understand it, where to place it, is how the thinking type functions most reflexively. This person's feeling life will come out in a more primitive, less sophisticated fashion.

---

[61] *Psychological Types,* CW 6.

[62] This discussion of typology is relatively superficial and the interested reader will want to see the works suggested in the select bibliography. Of the several tests to determine personality type, the simplest is to ask oneself which areas of life are easy and which difficult. The person who likes working on a car or keeping track of the checking balance will generally not enjoy reading speculative fiction. Similarly, the person who relates to people easily would have little interest in the solitary task of designing computer software.

During the Middle Passage the less developed parts of the psyche call for attention. Jung thought that Freud was a feeling type. He used his brilliant mind to develop a number of rationalizations to justify and defend his passionately held feelings. When his colleagues differed and departed, he considered them traitors to the cause. Rather than articulate his theories dispassionately and submit them to the marketplace of ideas, he used them to defend a feeling orientation to life. Jung, on the other hand, was an extraverted intuitive thinking type whose mind ranged over such topics as schizophrenia, alchemy and flying saucers. He had the "radiant thinking" of the intuitive but he lacked the sequential logic of the sensation type. To work on his sensation he cooked, sculpted and painted, all designed to bring the inferior function to consciousness.

At midlife we feel a lot of distress, much of it outer, much inner. Part of the inner distress originates from the fact that we, and our society, have colluded in neglecting the whole person. We have coasted on what was easy for us; we were rewarded for productivity not wholeness. In our dreams we live out the other side of the personality, for the inferior function is the trapdoor to the unconscious. If we are going to develop as individuals, and if we are going to enhance our relationships, we have to take seriously the issue of typology.

Jung's theory of typology is not just another way to put people in boxes. There are two major ways in which a knowledge of typology helps us. First, the single largest cause of conflict between persons is that they are operating from different typological orientations. The long-running Neil Simon play *The Odd Couple* had one joke with many variations, a joke based on pitting two opposing types against each other. Oscar and Felix processed reality in opposing ways, one seeing a messy room as a disturbance and the other as a place where everything is conveniently to hand, each convinced he was right and the other pig-headed. Interpersonal relationships, especially marriages, are notoriously troubled by differing typologies. Recognizing that the partner may be of another type enhances good will and can go a long way to reducing tension and misunderstanding.

Knowledge of one's dominant or superior function is also knowledge of one's inferior or inadequate orientation to reality. It tells us what aspects of our personality we need to develop, both for better adaptation to the outer world and for the balancing of the psyche. In concrete terms, we need to be able to perform those tasks which we generally avoid, often asking a spouse, for example, to cover for us.

In any relationship we are obliged to ask, "What am I expecting of this person which I ought to do for myself?" This question applies not only to the large emotional agenda of the inner child but to the issue of typology as well. Recognizing interdependence involves more than knowing who cuts the grass, who minds the check book and so on. It has to do with becoming a self-sufficient person who is free to celebrate the otherness of the Other.

During the Middle Passage it is useful to see how one's successes have also been imprisoning, constrictive to the whole person. Jogging and being active in sports, for instance, can be more than a means of managing stress. They can represent ways to get in touch with the sensate world again after spending a week at a desk. For the person who works manually, the life of the mind may call up the inferior function. At first one feels awkward using the less adapted processes, but in the end the psyche responds by a greater sense of grounded well-being. In our culture, one cannot count on the cooperation of employers or even family in this process of balancing one's psyche. All the more, then, must one steal time here and there. When hobbies are seen less as filling time than as feeding the soul, then we will likely be more serious in seeking alternatives to our usual way of functioning. Yet, apprehension about trying other than that which got us this far, may impede our desire to give energy to the neglected parts of the psyche, however potentially rewarding.

This is one aspect of the appointment we have with ourselves during the Middle Passage: to reclaim those parts of ourselves left behind through specialization, ignorance or prohibition. A consideration of typology is far more than an admonition to find a hobby. For many it is the only way to bring some balance back to a personality which has become too one-sided.

Shadow Invasions

Earlier we spoke of the enormous energy spent by the ego, in response to its socialization, to acquire a persona. The persona represents a necessary face to present to the outer world and it also protects our inner life. But just as the reliance on the superior function represents a partiality, so too is the persona a fragment of the Self. The persona is necessary in dealing with outer reality, but all the while the larger, unexplored psyche is waiting to be acknowledged.

The reader will recall that the shadow refers to everything in the individual that has been repressed. The more we have invested in a particular self-image, the more we have developed a one-sided adaptation to reality, and the more our sense of security is invested in what we have become at midlife, the more the invasions of the shadow are both necessary and disturbing.

Most of us are embarrassed about something we have done. Perhaps we fell into an affair, abused drugs or walked away from those who depended on us. Who has not awakened at four a.m. to find grinning demons at the foot of the bed? All our aberrant actions represent a blind groping for more life, for renewal, though their consequences may be damaging to ourselves and others. If we can be honest, we will discern our selfishness, our dependencies, our fears, our jealousies and even our capacity for destruction. Not a pretty picture, but one more rounded than our bright persona, more human. One of the wisest utterances by any human came from the Latin poet Terence who said, "Nothing human is alien to me."[63] This maxim hurts when we apply it to ourselves.

The shadow should not be equated with evil, only with life that has been suppressed. As such, the shadow is rich in potential. Becoming conscious of it makes us more fully human, more interesting. A shadowless person is extraordinarily bland and uninteresting. A willingness to allow our darkest impulses, as well as our repressed creativity, to surface and be acknowledged is a step toward their integration. Negative shadow contents such as rage, lust, anger, etc., can be destructive when acted out unconsciously, but when consciously acknowledged and channeled they can provide new directions and new energy.

In concrete terms, the shadow will out, whether in unconscious acts, projections onto others, depression or somatic illness.[64]

The shadow embodies all the life which has not been allowed expression. It embodies our lost sensitivity, which denied, breaks through in sentimentality. It represents our creativity, which abandoned, locks us into ennui and enervation. It embodies our spontaneity, which suppressed, routinizes and stultifies our lives. It represents a life force greater than our

---

[63] "Heauton Timorumenos," in *Comedies,* p. 77.

[64] An analyst friend of mine, who happens to be a priest, wrote his thesis on the founder of his order. In midlife, when the founder's early vision which led to the creation of the order became an entrapping institution, he sought to be relieved of his vows. When he was not, he became bed-ridden for the last twenty years of his life. Perhaps the shadow, his unlived life, took revenge.

conscious personality has yet utilized, and its blocking leads to diminished vitality.

A conscious appointment with the shadow at midlife is essential, for it will be operating surreptitiously in any case. We must examine what we envy or dislike in others and acknowledge those very things in ourselves. This helps to prevent our blaming or envying others for what we have not done ourselves. It encourages us to recognize that only a small part of our potential for life has been tapped and that we are often overly smug, overly secure in our ego achievements. It reveals other sources of energy, creativity and personal development. By dialoguing with our shadow we lift enormous projections of animosity or envy off of others. It is hard enough to live our own lives, and everyone is better served if we concentrate on our own individuation rather than getting stuck in the agendas of others.

If the meaning of life is directly related to the scope of consciousness and personal development, then the invasions of the shadow at midlife are necessary and potentially healing. The more I know about myself, the more of my potential I can incarnate, the more variegated the tones and hues of my personality will be and the richer my experience of life.

4

Case Studies in Literature

"Midway in life's journey, I found myself in a dark wood, having lost the way."[65] So begins Dante's spiritual pilgrimage, the revisioning of his life's meaning.

In this chapter I will discuss some literary cases rather than clinical examples. As Aristotle suggested twenty-five centuries ago, art can sometimes be clearer than life because art embraces the universal.[66] The artist's capacity to descend into the underworld, as Dante did, and to return bearing the story of the journey renders our condition in a particularly articulate fashion. We are called not only to identify with a particular character but also to see him or her as a dramatization of a universal human condition. Since we share that condition, we may learn something about ourselves from their limitations, insights and actions.

T. S. Eliot observed that our only superiority to the past is that we can contain it and be enlarged by it.[67] In other words, through literature and the arts we can contain more of the range of possibilities facing humans, and still have further capacity for growth and development. Hamlet, for example, will always have to say the lines written for Hamlet. We all suffer the Hamlet complex, namely times when we know we should do something but are unable to do it. Unlike Hamlet, we have the chance, through consciousness, to change the script.

Two quite disparate classics of the nineteenth century, Goethe's *Faust* at the beginning and Flaubert's *Madame Bovary* in the middle, dramatize the plight of the individual who sets off into the first adulthood full of projections and arrives at midlife to confusion, depression and the exhaustion of the strategies which got them that far.

The scholarly Faust embodies the Renaissance ideal, the acquisition of knowledge. He has mastered the professions of the time—law, philosophy, theology and medicine—"and here I am, for all my lore, / The wretched

---

[65] *The Comedy of Dante Alighieri,* p. 8.

[66] *Poetics,* p. 68.

[67] "Tradition and the Individual Talent," *Critical Theory Since Plato,* p. 78.

fool I was before."[68] Riding his dominant function, thinking, Faust has gained the apex of human learning and tastes not sweetness but ashes. How many CEOs have shared his disappointment? The more he has attained, the more his inferior function, feeling, has been suppressed. His feeling, as primitive in its expression as his thinking is sophisticated, comes roaring out and seizes him in a deep depression. His learning is impressive but his anima is oppressed. So great is his depression that more than once he considers suicide. He realizes that two souls contend within his breast, one which longs to make music that would melt the stars, and one tied to the banal and everyday. At that point of supreme tension, where a modern man would suffer a nervous breakdown, Faust is joined by Mephistopheles.

Mephistopheles is not evil in Goethe's version as much as he embodies Faust's shadow. "I am part of the part that once was everything, / Part of the darkness which gave birth to light."[69] Mephistopheles describes the shadow as that part of the whole, neglected and suppressed, which is necessary for the dialectic that ultimately brings wholeness.

Goethe's *Faust,* rich as it is, can be read many ways, one of which is as the midlife dialogue of the ego at midlife with its split-off parts. Pulled back from the brink of suicide, Faust makes a wager, not pact, with Mephistopheles; they will go forth on a magical tour of the world of experience, and because Faust represents the yearning of all humans for ever-increasing understanding, he says that Mephistopheles may have his soul if he is ever content, ever satiated in his journey.

As we know, what is unconscious is suffered inwardly or projected outwardly. Initially in a state of suicidal depression, Faust's encounter with the shadowy Mephistopheles is an opportunity for renewal. But he must first go within and experience all that has been repressed in his one-sided first adulthood.

The central encounter which Faust suffers is the overdue meeting with his anima, the inner feminine, the locus of feeling, instinctual truth and joy, in the outer form of a simple peasant girl named Margaret. She is stunned by the interest of this scholar of world renown and he too is smitten. He describes her with terms generally reserved for religious endearment. The enthusiasm of his love for her is adolescent in character, sug-

---

[68] *Faust,* p. 93.
[69] Ibid., p. 161.

gesting where the development of the anima was blocked in the education of the scholar. The complexity of their affair leads to a poisoned mother and a murdered brother, and Margaret's mind breaks under the burden. Faust, guilt-ridden, is led off by Mephistopheles to explore the larger world.[70]

This superficial plot summary smacks of a soap opera with Faust as the villain. Indeed, he is far from innocent in the seduction and ruination of Margaret, but the level of his unconsciousness and the implications for change at midlife are our concern here. In these terms, the narrative reveals a person who has developed the dominant function, his intellect, at the expense of his shadow and his anima. The penumbra of the shadow crossing the anima is disastrous, as midlife affairs often are. What we do not know does hurt us, and others. Faust is not unethical, but in his unconsciousness he is destructive.

There is no reason to believe that each part of a person matures in unison. Western society has leaped forward in its capacity for nuclear destruction and medical prolongation of life, but our ethical maturation has lagged behind. So, too, Faust develops his role in the outer world most successfully, but the inner life is neglected. His anima is unconscious and primitive compared to his intellect, so she appears as a simple peasant girl. The urge for renewal, which initially takes a quasi-religious form, is really the need to bring the neglected feminine into consciousness. How difficult it is for any of us to recognize that what is demanded is inner healing. It is so much easier to seek solace or satisfaction in the outer world.

Faust's dilemma is reminiscent of a short story by the modern American writer John Cheever, "The Country Husband." A businessman survives a plane crash and finds his suburban life turned upside down. The whiff of his mortality stirs his anima. He snaps at his wife and her friends, falls in love with his adolescent baby-sitter and toddles off to therapy, where he is told he is suffering from a midlife crisis. The diagnosis complete, he is given a hobby and at story's end is working with wood in his basement. Inside him, nothing is resolved, nothing learned or integrated, and the planets whirl through space unchanged in their orbits.

Both Faust and Cheever's protagonist are ambushed at midlife by depression and the fear of death; both seek the healing of the anima through a

---

[70] For a full-length psychological study, see Edward F. Edinger, *Goethe's Faust: Notes for a Jungian Commentary*.

young girl. Both suffer and neither learns what it is all about. As Jung said, neurosis is suffering which has not discovered its meaning. Keeping our appointment with midlife involves both the suffering and the search for its meaning. Then growth is possible.

Emma Bovary, in Flaubert's book, is that peasant girl. When she sees Charles Bovary, a local physician, she campaigns to ensnare him and move from the farm to his small town. She projects onto marriage and position her salvation from ordinariness. But soon after they marry she is pregnant and bored with her pedestrian husband. Trapped by the limitations of her culture, nineteenth-century Catholic France, she can neither abort nor divorce, nor can she strike off on her own as Ibsen's Nora would decades later. She whiles away her time reading romantic novels, the equivalent of today's soap operas, and fantasizes about lovers who will take her out of the banal into the world of smart people. She goads Charles into a complicated surgery which ends in disaster, undertakes a series of affairs and borrows to support her wistful spending sprees. Her animus development, first projected onto Charles, wanders from man to man in a romantic fantasy of rescue. Like Faust she seeks transcendence from her limitations without understanding that she must work from within.

The more unconscious we are, the more we project. Emma's life is a series of escalating projections, each failing to satisfy. She even finds in adultery "all the platitudes of marriage."[71] Finally, abandoned by lovers, at the brink of financial ruin and despairing of finding the man of her dreams, Emma plans to take her life. Her novels have told her how heroines are transported to heaven, attended by angels and celestial music. She takes poison to bring the final transcendence, the final projection. Flaubert cuts through the haze: "At eight o'clock the vomiting began . . ."[72] Her final vision is not beatific, it is the face of a blind man. The beggar she once passed en route to an assignation reappears, symbolizing the blindness of the inner man, her animus.

Neither Faust nor Emma is evil. The urgency of their unlived lives causes them to make bad choices. They project their inner contrasexual onto an outer person, not realizing that what they seek is ultimately within. While their stories are uniquely wrought by great artists, the lineaments of their Middle Passage are common to us all.

---

[71] *Madame Bovary,* p. 211.

[72] Ibid., p. 230.

A midlife encounter of quite a different sort occurs in Dostoevsky's *Notes from Underground*. Published in 1864, it is an indictment of the cult of progress, of meliorism, of naive optimism about the capacity of Reason to eradicate the world's woes. But even more than an analysis of the modern Zeitgeist, it represents a profoundly searing encounter with the shadow. Few have written of the inner darkness with such honesty or such depth of insight as has Dostoevsky.

Notes from Underground begins with some lyrical lines not quite typical of Victorian literary affectation: "I'm a sick man . . . a mean man. . . . But, actually, I don't understand a damn thing about my sickness; I'm not even too sure what it is that's ailing me." The unnamed speaker plunges into a narcissistic monologue: "Now then, what does a decent man like to talk about most? Himself, of course. So I'll talk about myself." And so in the pages that follow he depicts his fears, his projections, his rage, his jealousies, those all-too-human traits one tends to deny, noting slyly that "people do pride themselves on their infirmities and I, probably, more than anyone."[73]

The Underground Man makes conscious what all of us do in the first adulthood, namely, react to life's wounds. We build a set of wound-based behaviors and live out our handicapped vision with rationalizations and self-justification. But the Underground Man will not indulge himself, or us, with rationalizations. The reader wants to see him in a better light, for his self-indictment implicates the rest of us. But, as he says, "How can a man with my lucidity of perception respect himself?"[74] He defines humanity as "the ungrateful biped. But this is still not his main defect. His main defect is his chronic perversity."[75]

The Underground Man refuses to make himself lovable or forgivable. He refuses to let himself or the reader off the hook. His self-analysis does not make for pleasant reading, but he presciently calls himself the first of the antiheroes.[76] He is heroic in his perversity and his honesty obliges the reader to a similar inventory. Thus he admonishes:

> All I did was carry to the limit what you haven't dared to push even halfway—taking your cowardice for reasonableness, thus making your-

---

[73] *Notes from Underground,* pp. 90-93.

[74] Ibid., p. 101.

[75] Ibid., p. 113.

[76] Ibid., p. 202.

selves feel better. So I may still turn out to be more *alive* than you in the end.[77]

Kafka once wrote that a great work should be as an axe to break the frozen sea within us.[78] *Notes from Underground* is such a work. Some still question its literary value and see it primarily as an indictment of an age of shallow optimism. But we can also view *Notes from Underground* as the effort of a person to keep his appointment with himself at midlife. While encounters with the shadow are not uncommon in literature, from Hawthorne to Melville, to Poe, to Twain, to Stevenson's Jeckyl and Hyde, to Conrad's *Heart of Darkness*, Dostoevsky takes us into the belly of the beast. He delineates the inferior regions which one has so strenuously sought to conceal. However, the greater the effort to suppress and split off the rich, loamy shadow, the more it breaks through in projections and dangerous acting out, as we see in Faust and Emma Bovary.

As painful as the encounter with our shadow may be, it reconnects us with our humanity. It contains the raw energy of life which, if handled consciously, can lead to change and renewal. Certainly it is hard to convert narcissism into something useful, but at least it may be contained and others spared injury. In the words of his contemporary, Charles Baudelaire, the Underground man is *"mon semblable, mon frère."*[79]

The person whose *vocatus* is art works and reworks his or her myth, sometimes consciously, sometimes unconsciously. The great poet W.B. Yeats went through numerous transformations. Apparently, some friends complained at one juncture about the new poet emerging when they had just become used to the old. His response:

> The friends have it I do wrong
> Whenever I remake my song
> Should know what issue is at stake.
> It is myself that I remake.[80]

The three poets who follow represent self-conscious efforts to rework one's personal myth. As the great myths of mace and miter, the anchoring power of throne and church, have receded, individuals have been left to find

---

[77] Ibid, p. 203.

[78] *Selected Short Stories of Franz Kafka*, p. xx.

[79] *An Anthology of French Poetry from Nerval to Valery in English Translation*, p. 295.

[80] See Richard Ellman, *Yeats: The Man and the Masks*, p. 186.

their own way through the wasteland. Much of modern art is testimony to our need to pick through the rubble of the past, choosing here and there a cloak of symbols which still fits, but mostly aimed at extracting meaning from personal experience. If the spiritual wellsprings of the past are generally unavailable for the artist today, then he or she will have to draw the longitudes and latitudes of the soul from the shards of biography. Of those shards, the most important are generally mother and father, the childhood milieu and acculturation. In the last chapter we saw Stephen Dunn working with the mother and father complexes. Three other modern American poets—Theodore Roethke, Richard Hugo and Diane Wakoski—also sift through the thesaurus of memory, seeking to piece together a coherent sense of self.

As we have seen, our two most compelling needs are for nurturance and empowerment, the feeling that life somehow serves and succors us and that we can achieve our goals. Theodore Roethke spent his childhood in Saginaw, Michigan, where his father owned a greenhouse. It served as the locus for many of his poems, for it came to symbolize not only his literal home but an Edenic memory of "the green world." Parental figures are the vehicles through whom the archetypal forces of nurturance and empowerment are transmitted. When the parent is able to carry those large forces and pass them on, they become activated within the child. Failing to find these forces in the personal parent, the child will seek them in surrogates. Here Roethke recalls after many years three employees of his father who helped fill the archetypal needs of the child:

> Gone the three ancient ladies
> Who creaked on the greenhouse ladders,
> Reaching up white strings
> To wind, to wind
> The sweet-pea tendrils, the smilax,
> Nasturtiums, the climbing
> Roses, to straighten
> Carnations, red
> Chrysanthemums; the stiff
> Stems, jointed like corn,
> They tied and tucked,—
> These nurses of nobody else.
> Quicker than birds, they dipped
> Up and sifted the dirt;
> They sprinkled and shook;
> They stood astride pipes,

Their skirts billowing out wide into tents,
Their hands twinkling with wet;
Like witches they flew along rows
Keeping creation at ease;
With a tendril for needle
They sewed up the air with a stem;
They teased out the seed that the cold kept asleep,—
All the coils, loops, and whorls.
They trellised the sun; they plotted for more than themselves.

I remember how they picked me up, a spindly kid,
Pinching and poking my thin ribs
Till I lay in their laps, laughing,
Weak as a wiffet;
Now, when I'm alone and cold in my bed,
They still hover over me,
These ancient leathery crones,
With their bandannas stiffened with sweat,
And their thorn-bitten wrists,
And their snuff-laden breath blowing lightly over me
   in my first sleep.[81]

The three women, frozen in time as a fly in amber, still nurture the child within. Their work, and their care for the child, seem now to provide a temenos, a sacred place in the psyche, while the poet has gone through difficult times fighting depression and loss. More than employees, they were nurses of growing things, be they plant or child. His memory revives the wonder of such simple things—billowing skirts, witchlike movements, sweat-stiffened bandannas, thorn-bitten wrists, snuff-laden breath— all metonymies which open into the past. In a difficult present, alone and cold, the writer reconnects with a nurturant, greening time. Memory serves to sustain, even to feed, the hungry soul. And just so, our own confrontation at midlife with the largeness of life, the loneliness of the journey, may be partially mediated by the connection with a time when life did support and sustain.

Richard Hugo has a tougher time finding that green memory:

You remember the name was Jensen. She seemed old,
always alone inside, face pasted gray to the window,
and mail never came. Two blocks down, the Grubskis

---

[81] "Frau Bauman, Frau Schmidt, and Frau Schwartze," in *The Collected Poems of Theodore Roethke*, p. 144.

went insane. George played rotten trombone
Easter when they flew the flag. Wild roses
remind you the roads were unpaved, gravel and vacant lots
the rule. Poverty was real, wallet and spirit,
and each day slow as church. You remember threadbare
church groups on the corner, howling their faith
at stars, and the violent Holy Rollers
renting the barn for their annual violent sing
and the barn burned down when you came back from war.
Knowing the people you knew then are dead,
you try to believe these roads paved are improved,
the neighbors, moved in while you were away, good-looking,
their dogs well fed. You still have need
to remember lots empty and fern.
Lawns well trimmed remind you of the train
your wife took one day forever, some far empty town,
the odd name you never recall. The time: 6:23.
The day: October 9. The year remains a blur.
You blame this neighborhood for your failure.
In some vague way, the Grubskis degraded you
beyond repair. And you know you must play again
and again Mrs. Jensen pale at her window, must hear
the foul music over the good slide of traffic.
You loved them well and they remain, still with nothing
to do, no money and no will. Loved them, and the gray
that was their disease you carry for extra food
in case you're stranded in some odd empty town
and need hungry lovers for friends, and need feel
you are welcome in the secret club they have formed.[82]

Childhood for Hugo was lived out on mean streets, where poverty of purse and poverty of spirit were allied. For the child time rolled in a slow crawl and yet so quickly that it seems difficult to account for all the changes since. Progress has come. Streets are paved, lawns and pets well fed. But other images float in an out of that strange novel we call our lives. People, some of them kin, some kin and not kind, have come and gone and the only continuity is the mind of the one trying to make sense of it all. Somehow, the poet feels, the locus of childhood, the neighborhood itself, set things in motion.

If the poet thinks of his or her life as a failure, then the point of origin,

---

[82] "What Thou Lovest Well, Remains American," in *Making Certain It Goes On: The Collected Poems of Richard Hugo*, p. 48.

the place of setting forth, is also implicated, degrading the pristine promise of childhood. Yet Hugo, like Roethke, in darker days still returns to his place of departure to get some clue as to who he is and what his life represents. Even now, "the gray / that was their disease you carry for extra food." One can scarce travel the long journey toward the unknown without resources. Since we know that friends and lovers have their own journey and can travel only part of the way with us, the poet is obliged to carry the shards of memory as soul food.

Hugo and Roethke are both members of that "secret club" referred to in the last line of the above poem. It is the community of those who are at the end of their resources and are obliged to regroup, get their mythic bearings. James Hillman has pointed out that all case histories are fictions.[83] The facts of one's life are far less important than how we remember them, how we have internalized them and are driven by them, or how we are able to work with them.

Every night the myth-making process is at work as our unconscious stirs up the detritus of daily life. So, too, memory serves to sustain, to anchor us to infantility, or to deceive us, as the case may be. Returning to the scenes of childhood, literally or imaginatively, helps one establish an adult relationship to that alleged reality. Visit the third grade classroom and the desks which dwarfed the child, the forbidding corridors, the endless playground—all are reduced in proportion. So, too, the traumas of the past may be assimilated by the adult who takes the inner child in hand and allows the gigantic pains or pleasures of memory to be reworked by the strength and knowledge of the adult.

The only requisite to entry into the Middle Passage is to have discovered that one does not know who one is, that there are no rescuers, no Mommy or Daddy, and that one's fellow travelers will do well to survive themselves. When one acknowledges one's arrival at this pivotal juncture, one may then be able to work through the warp and weft of one's life to find which threads lead from then to now.

Diane Wakoski seeks to find out who she is by examining emulsified images of her past:

> My sister in her well-tailored silk blouse hands me
> the photo of my father
> in naval uniform and white hat.

---

83 *Healing Fiction.*

I say, "Oh, this is the one which Mama used to have on her
    dresser."

My sister controls her face and furtively looks at my mother,
a sad rag bag of a woman, lumpy and sagging everywhere,
like a mattress at the Salvation Army, though with no holes or
    tears,
and says, "No."

I look again,
and see that my father is wearing a wedding ring,
which he never did
when he lived with my mother. And that there is a legend on it,
"To my dearest wife,
    Love
    Chief"
And I realize the photo must have belonged to his second wife,
whom he left our mother to marry.

My mother says, with her face as still as the whole unpopulated
    part of the
state of North Dakota,
"May I see it too?"
She looks at it.

I look at my tailored sister
and my own blue-jeaned self. Have we wanted to hurt our
    mother,
sharing these pictures on this, one of the few days I ever visit or
spend with family? For her face is curiously haunted,
not now with her usual viperish bitterness,
but with something so deep it could not be spoken.

I turn away and say I must go on, as I have a dinner engagement
    with friends.
But I drive all the way to Pasadena from Whittier,
thinking of my mother's face; how I could never love her; how
    my father
could not love her either. Yet knowing I have inherited
the rag-bag body,
stony face with bulldog jaws.

I drive, thinking of that face.
Jeffers' California Medea who inspired me to poetry.
I killed my children,
but there as I am changing lanes on the freeway, necessarily
    glancing in the

rearview mirror, I see the face,
not even a ghost, but always with me, like a photo in a beloved's
    wallet.

How I hate my destiny.[84]

    Photos, unlike the easeful balm of forgetfulness, pull memory up and
out of the unconscious. The three women—mother, sister and poet—are
pulled together through the picture of the past. Beneath the surface lurk old
wounds and old tensions. The poet skates across time as a child steps on
the pond's ice, not knowing what will hold, what betray, but must still
try to walk across. In another poem, Wakoski tells how she "adopted"
George Washington as her father, since her biological parent was "30 years
a chief petty officer, / always away from home."[85] She adopts the man
who lived in the past at Mt. Vernon and still on dollar bills and in the
child's memory, for "my father made me what I am, / a lonely woman, /
without a purpose, / just as I was a lonely child / without any father."[86]
    Wakoski's experience of her mother, like Hugo's of his old neighbor-
hood, is like a Salvation Army mattress, empty as North Dakota and
viperish to boot. Her sibling, well tailored, contrasts with her own "blue-
jeaned self." As she drives home to wherever home is, she knows she trav-
els alone. All of them—the Chief Petty Officer, mother, sister, poet—are
solitary sojourners. Unlike Roethke, who can draw sustenance still from
the three greenhouse crones, or Hugo, who can even sup from the dismal
greyness, Wakoski knows she cannot draw strength or comfort or nurturance from the times or people the photos depict. She confesses she could
not love her mother, nor could the Chief Petty Officer. Yet she carries her
mother's imago, on the face in the rear-view mirror, in her image of herself. She has traveled from Pasadena to Whittier and sundry soulscapes beyond, but her mother's imprint stares back at her, always.
    Like another cursed and tragic woman, Medea, she has slain what was
potential within her. Driven by the wounded vision of self, she has created
her life. The more she tried to get away from Pasadena past, the more it
has insinuated itself into her. "How I hate my destiny," she concludes.
    It is essential that we distinguish here between fate and destiny, as
Athenian tragedians did twenty-five centuries ago. The poet did not choose

---

84 "The Photos," in *Emerald Ice: Selected Poems 1962-87,* pp. 295-296.
85 "The Father of My Country," ibid., p. 44.
86 Ibid, p. 48.

her parents, to be sure, as they did not choose her. But, suffering the fate of their intersection in time and space, each wounds the others. Out of such wounds we create that assemblage of behaviors and attitudes which serve to protect the fragile child. That assemblage, reinforced through the years, becomes the acquired personality, the false self. Wakoski rightly returns to her roots to discern how she was set in motion. What she sees, however, repulses her, for staring back from the mirror is the same woman neither she nor the Chief Petty Officer could love. As long as she is only the reflection of what she cannot love, she cannot love herself. Destiny, however, is not the same as fate. Destiny represents one's potential, inherent possibilities which may or may not come to fruition. Destiny invites choice. Destiny without choice is only fate replicated. Her struggle to be more than that which she grew to hate still ties her to what she disdains and disowns. As long as she defines herself as her mother's daughter, she is tied to her fate. While the poem does not, within its borders, offer much hope of transcending fate, on the other hand the self-examination inherent in creating the poem represents the necessary act of consciousness and personal responsibility which makes destiny possible.

Without painful efforts toward consciousness one stays wound-identified. In Sylvia Plath's well-known confessional poem "Daddy," she recalls her professor father standing at the blackboard and suddenly equates him with a devil who "bit my pretty red heart in two," adding "at twenty I tried to die / and get back, back, back to you."[87] Her father's crime was to have died when she was ten, at the point her animus needed him to free her from mother-dependency. Like Wakoski, she was left by Him, left with Her, stuck at the point of wounding. Plath's rage and self-hatred pulled her back and down repeatedly until finally she ended her life. When one stays wound-identified one will hate the face in the mirror for its similarity to those responsible for the wounding, and feel self-hate for one's failure to break free of the past.

Artists often tell us more, through their ability to articulate the universal, than do biographical facts. "Memory," Apollonaire wrote, "is a hunting horn whose sound dies out along the wind."[88] Our biographies are traps, deceptive enticements that freeze us in the seeming facticity of the

---

[87] "Ariel," *The Collected Poems,* p. 42.

[88] *An Anthology of French Poetry from Nerval to Valery in English Translation,* p. 252.

past, wound-identified and creatures of fate.

In the secret club of the Middle Passage, there is an invitation for greater consciousness and an enlarged capacity for choice. With greater consciousness comes a greater opportunity for forgiveness of others and of ourselves, and, with forgiveness, release from the past. We must address the making of our myths more consciously or we shall never be more than the sum of what has happened to us.

5

Individuation:
Jung's Myth for Our Time

The experience of the Middle Passage is not unlike awakening to find that one is alone on a pitching ship, with no port in sight. One can only go back to sleep, jump ship or grab the wheel and sail on.

At the moment of decision, the high adventure of the soul is never more clear. In grabbing the wheel we take responsibility for the journey, however frightening it might be, however lonely or unfair it may seem. In not grabbing the wheel, we stay stuck in the first adulthood, stuck in the neurotic aversions which constitute our operant personality and, therefore, our self-estrangement. At no point do we live more honestly, or with more integrity, than when, surrounded by others yet knowing oneself to be alone, the journey of the soul beckons and we say "yes" to it all. That is when, as a character in a play by Christopher Fry says, "Affairs have become soul-sized, thank God!"[89]

In his autobiography Jung writes:

> I have frequently seen people become neurotic when they content themselves with inadequate or wrong answers to the questions of life. They seek position, marriage, reputation, outward success or money, and remain unhappy and neurotic even when they have attained what they were seeking. Such people are usually confined within too narrow a spiritual horizon. Their life has not sufficient content, sufficient meaning. If they are enabled to develop into more spacious personalities, the neurosis generally disappears.[90]

Jung's point is essential, for all of us have lived lives constrained within the narrow confines of our own time, place and personal history. To live a more abundant life we are obliged to understand the limits within which we were raised. The implicit premise of our culture, that through materialism, narcissism or hedonism we would be happy, is clearly bankrupt. Those who have embraced such values are not happy or complete.

---

[89] *A Sleep of Prisoners,* p. 43.
[90] *Memories, Dreams, Reflections,* p. 140.

What we need is not unexamined "truths" but living myth, that is, a structure of value which guides the soul's energies in a way that is consistent with our nature. While it is often useful to pick through the rubble of the past for images which speak to us as individuals, rarely is it possible to wholly embrace the mythologies of another time and place. We are obliged to find our own.

The necessity of finding our path is obvious, but major obstacles stand in the way. Let us review for a moment the symptoms characteristic of the midlife transition. They are boredom, repeated job or partner shifts, substance abuse, self-destructive thoughts or acts, infidelity, depression, anxiety and growing compulsivity. Behind these symptoms there are two fundamental truths. The first is that there is an enormous force pressing from below. Its urgency is felt as disruptive, causing anxiety when acknowledged and depression when suppressed. The second fundamental truth is that the old patterns which kept such inner urgency at bay are repeated with growing anxiety but decreasing efficacy. Changing one's job or relationship does not change one's sense of oneself over the long run. When increasing pressure from within becomes less and less containable by the old strategies, a crisis of selfhood erupts. We do not know who we are, really, apart from social roles and psychic reflexes. And we do not know what to do to lessen the pressure.

Such symptoms announce the need for substantive change in a person's life. Suffering quickens consciousness, and from new consciousness new life may follow. The task is daunting, for one must first acknowledge that there is no rescue, no parent to make everything better and no way to go back to an earlier time. The Self has sought growth by exhausting the tired strategies of the ego. The ego structure which one worked so hard to create is now revealed to be petty, frightened and out of answers. At midlife the Self maneuvers the ego assemblage into crisis in order to bring about a correction of course.

Underlying the symptoms that typify the Middle Passage is the assumption that we shall be saved by finding and connecting with someone or something new in the outer world. Alas, for the drowning midlife sailor there are no such life preservers. We are in the sea-surge of the soul, along with many others to be sure, but needing to swim under our own power. The truth is simply that what we must know will come from within. If we can align our lives with that truth, no matter how difficult the abrasions of the world, we will feel healing, hope and new life. The experience of early childhood, and later of our culture, alienated us from ourselves. We can only get back on course by reconnecting with our inner truths.

In December of 1945 an Arab peasant found a number of ancient manuscripts buried in large jars within caves. These manuscripts seem to have been the texts of the gnostics, early Christians who relied more on personal, revealed experience than on official pronouncements of the church. One of those manuscripts was titled "The Gospel According to Thomas." Reportedly, it contains the secret sayings of Jesus and if that is so they reveal a much different person from the one revealed by the other disciples. One of Jesus' utterances exactly addresses the point we must accept if we are to undergo transformation at midlife. He said, "If you bring forth what is within you, what you bring forth will save you. If you do not bring forth what is within you, what you do not bring forth will destroy you."[91]

Because what is within has been suppressed, we are ill and self-alienated. Because what is within has been so little affirmed, we have great difficulty in knowing that what we have sought all along, the path which is right for us, has been there. While it is frightening to contemplate the largeness of the task, it is also liberating in an ultimate sense to know that one has the necessary resources within and is not dependent on another to live one's life fully. As the Romantic poet Hölderlin wrote nearly two centuries ago, "The gods are near but difficult to grasp; where danger is greatest, however, deliverance grows stronger."[92]

It is not, then, a matter of living without myth, but rather which myth, for we are always guided by images, consciously or unconsciously. Consciously we may subscribe to a set of beliefs and practices which accord with collective values, like the pursuit of wealth or acceding to group norms, but the price of such accommodation is neurosis. Or we may be living out a false myth such as, "I must forever be the good child, eschewing anger and serving others." Such a guiding imago may be so deeply unconscious that one has always reacted that way and can hardly conceive of another. Neither outer conformity nor inner compliance supports wholeness. Indeed, one is repeatedly enjoined to serve the Outer, and when the collision occurs, to continue service to the programmed expectations. Again, the stability of the society is served, but at the cost of the individ-

---

[91] Elaine Pagels, *The Gnostic Gospels,* p. 152.
[92] "Patmos," in *An Anthology of German Poetry from Hölderlin to Rilke,* p. 34.

ual. In his 1939 speech to the Guild for Pastoral Psychology in London, Jung noted that we are forced to choose between outer ideologies or private neurosis. Only the path of individuation could serve as a viable alternative.[93] This is still true.

The concept of individuation represents Jung's myth for our time in the sense of a set of images which guide the soul's energies. Simply put, individuation is the developmental imperative of each of us to become ourselves as fully as we are able, within the limits imposed on us by fate. Again, unless we consciously confront our fate, we are tied to it. We must separate who we are from what we have acquired, our de facto but false sense of self. "I am not what happened to me; I am what I choose to become." This sentence must be conscious to us each day if we are to become more than prisoners of our fate. This dilemma, and the necessity of consciousness, has been expressed rather humorously in the anonymous "Autobiography in Five Short Chapters":

I

I walk down the street.
   There is a deep hole in the sidewalk.
   I fall in.
   I am lost . . . I am helpless
      It isn't my fault.
   It takes forever to find a way out.

II

I walk down the same street.
There is a deep hole in the sidewalk.
   I pretend I don't see it.
   I fall in again.
I can't believe I am in this same place.
      But it isn't my fault.
It still takes a long time to get out.

III

I walk down the same street.
There is a deep hole in the sidewalk.
   I see it is there.
   I still fall in . . . it's a habit . . . but,
      my eyes are open.
      I know where I am.

---

93 "The Symbolic Life," *The Symbolic Life,* CW 18, pars 632, 673-674.

It is *my* fault.
I get out immediately.

IV

I walk down the same street.
There is a deep hole in the sidewalk.
I walk around it.

V

I walk down another street.

We will never know for certain how free or determined we really are, but we are obliged, as the existentialists reminded us, to act as if we were free. Such action restores dignity and purpose to the person who otherwise would continue to suffer only as a victim. Leaving New York, a pilot who corrects the course of a 747 only a few degrees will arrive either in Europe or Africa. So we, with even minor correctives, can effect huge changes in our lives. To take on this project there is no escape from a daily commitment to stay in touch with what comes to us from within. As Jung has explained, the individual

> has an *a priori* unconscious existence, but exists consciously only so far as a consciousness of his peculiar nature is present. . . . A conscious process of differentiation, or individuation, is needed to bring the individuality to consciousness, i.e., to raise it out of the state of identity with the object.[94]

The identity with the object to which Jung refers is one's identification initially with the reality with the parent, and later with the authority of the parent complexes and the institutions of society. As long as we remain primarily identified with the outer, objective world, we will be estranged from our subjective reality. Of course we are always social beings, but we are also spiritual beings with a *telos* or mysterious end of our own. While maintaining fidelity to outer relationships, we must become more fully the person we were meant to be. Indeed, the more differentiated we become as individuals, the more enriched will be our relationships. So Jung argues,

> As the individual is not just a single, separate being, but by his very existence presupposes a collective relationship, it follows that the process of individuation must lead to more intense and broader collec-

---

[94] "Definitions," *Psychological Types,* CW 6, par. 755.

tive relationships and not to isolation.[95]

The paradox of individuation is that we best serve intimate relationship by becoming sufficiently developed in ourselves that we do not need to feed off others. Similarly, we best serve our society by being individuals, by contributing to the dialectic necessary for the health of any group. Each chip in the social mosaic contributes best by the richness of its own unique coloration. We remain most socially useful when we have something unique, our fullest possible selves, to offer. Jung again:

> Individuation cuts one off from personal conformity and hence from collectivity. That is the guilt which the individuant leaves behind him for the world, that is the guilt he must endeavor to redeem. He must offer a ransom in place of himself, that is, he must bring forth values which are an equivalent substitute for his absence in the collective personal sphere.[96]

Thus, a concern for individuation is not narcissistic; it is the best way to serve society and support the individuation of others. The world is not served by those who are alienated from themselves and others, nor by those who in their pain bring pain to others. Individuation, as a set of guiding images which constitute the goal and the process at the same time, serves the person who in turn contributes to the culture. "The goal is important only as an idea," writes Jung, "the essential thing is the *opus* which leads to the goal: *that* is the goal of a lifetime."[97]

When we grasp the wheel on the captain's deck, scarce knowing our direction, knowing only that the thing must be done, then we live the high adventure of the soul. In the long run, it is the only journey worth taking. The task of the first half of life is to attain sufficient ego strength to leave parents and enter the world. This strength becomes available in the second half for the larger journey of the soul. Then the axis shifts from ego-world to ego-Self and the mystery of life unfolds in ever renewing ways. This is not a denial of our social reality but a restoration of the essentially religious character of our lives. Hence Jung suggested that we must ask of a person,

---

[95] Ibid., par. 758.

[96] "Adaptation, Individuation, Collectivity," *The Symbolic Life,* CW 18, par. 1095.

[97] "The Psychology of the Transference," *The Practice of Psychotherapy,* CW 16, par. 400.

Is he related to something infinite or not? That is the telling question of his life. . . . If we understand and feel that here in this life we already have a link with the infinite, desires and attitudes change. In the final analysis, we count for something only because of the essential we embody, and if we do not embody that, life is wasted.[98]

The capacity to stand in relationship to that which is larger than our ego is to be informed and transformed by it. Over the entrance to the Temple of Apollo at Delphi the priests inscribed the admonition, "Know Thyself." According to an ancient text the entrance to the inner chamber had the collateral inscription, "Thou Art." These injunctions capture the individuation dialectic well. We are to know ourselves more fully and to know ourselves in the context of the larger mystery.

---

[98] *Memories, Dreams, Reflections,* p. 325.

6

On the High Seas and Alone

Each of us is called to individuate, though not all will hear or heed. If we do not tend to our own process, our own journey, we risk denying the life forces which led to our incarnation and losing our sense of meaning. As long as we are on the high seas of the soul anyway, why not be as conscious and as courageous as possible?

This final chapter presents a series of attitudes and practices which anyone can employ. The usefulness of a formal therapeutic relationship notwithstanding, what follows is for those who may not choose to enter therapy as well as for those who do.

From Loneliness to Solitude

The American poet Marianne Moore once wrote that "the best cure for loneliness is solitude."[99] What does she mean? What is the difference between loneliness and solitude?

Loneliness is not a contemporary discovery, nor is the flight from it. The seventeenth-century philosopher Blaise Pascal observed in his *Pensées* that the jester was invented to divert the king from loneliness for, king though he may be, if he think of self he would grow vexed and anxious. So, Pascal argued, all of modern culture was a vast *divertissement* to keep us from loneliness and from thinking of self.[100] Similarly, Nietzsche wrote a hundred years ago, "When we are alone and quiet we are afraid that something will be whispered in our ear, and so we hate the silence and drug ourselves with social life."[101]

One cannot begin to heal or engage one's own soulfulness without a keen appreciation of the relationship to the Self. To achieve this requires solitude, that psychic state wherein one is wholly present to oneself. Following are some of the issues which must be confronted if one is to move from loneliness to solitude.

---

[99] *The Complete Prose of Marianne Moore*, p. 96.
[100] *Pensées*, p. 39.
[101] *The Portable Nietzsche*, p. 164.

Absorbing the trauma of separation

It is difficult to fully appreciate either the trauma of birth, which is a primal separation, or the full effects of the parent-child relationship. The more beneficent that relationship, the more one will be self-sufficient and comfortable with solitude. Paradoxically, the more troubled the relationship to the parent, the more dependent the person will be on relationships in general. The more volatile the parental environment, the more one learns self-definition only in terms of the Other. Jung put parents in a difficult spot when he wrote that they "should always be conscious of the fact that they themselves are the principal cause of neurosis in their children."[102] This is cited here not to instill guilt in parents, but to remind us of just how much we have been defined by them and by parent substitutes such as social institutions.

To move to the necessary solitude in which individuation can proceed, one must consciously ask each day, "In what way am I so afraid that I am avoiding myself, my own journey?" The codependent adult has learned to avoid his or her own being. The cliché "to get in touch with one's feelings" really asks us to define ourselves from an inner reality rather than an outer context. We must further ask of our responses to others, "Where is the parent lurking here?" Then we may operate out of personal integrity. The more traumatic the childhood, the more infantile our sense of reality. It is very hard to know our reality and to operate from its baseline. Risking loneliness to achieve that sense of oneness with oneself we call solitude is essential if one is to survive the Middle Passage.

Loss and the withdrawal of projections

Great losses often occur at midlife: children move away, a friend dies, divorce devastates. The loss of that necessary Other can be as existentially terrifying as the loss of the parent would be to the child. The adult feels not only angst but a loss of identity. (A popular song laments, "Can't live if living is without you . . .") What this tells us is how much of our lives have been caught up in the projections of meaning and identity onto the Other, be it spouse, child or persona. Yes, some people feel liberated by a divorce or the departure of a child, but many do not. What is essential is to honor the relationship by feeling its loss, and yet recognize that one has

---

[102] "Introduction to Wickes's 'Analyse der Kinderseele,' " *The Development of Personality,* CW 17, par. 84.

had, all along, a commitment larger than any single relationship.

A person who has suffered loss and the withdrawal of projections will have struggled with the dependencies which haunt us all, but also will have asked the next question, "How much of the unknown me was tied up in that person or that role?" When we can acknowledge loss and recoup the energy that was once invested outside ourselves, it becomes available for the next stage of the journey.

Ritualizing fear

People so fear loneliness that they will cling to terrible relationships and constricting professions rather than risk the consequences of letting go of the Other. In the end, there is no substitute for the courage necessary to confront loneliness. The something Nietzsche suggested we feared hearing may be useful and liberating. But we will never hear that inner voice unless we risk solitude. For some, it helps to devise a daily ritual of private meaning which obliges one to sit quietly, with no phone, no children, nothing, and listen to the silence. Such a ritual may at first seem strained and artificial, but sticking to it will allow the silence to speak. When we are not lonely in being alone, then we have achieved solitude. Fear keeps us from this essential meeting with ourselves.

The purpose of a ritual is to link a person to the larger rhythms of life. As they are passed from generation to generation, rituals become routine and lose their original power. All the more reason, then, for the individual to generate a ritual of personal significance, investing it with the same energy previously given to dependencies. The goal is to still the traffic of the mind, the neurotic clutter which floods and distracts. If we are afraid of being alone, afraid of silence, then we can never really be present to ourselves. Self-alienation is very much the condition of the modern world and it can only be changed by individual action.

So, some part of every day, it is good to risk radical presence to oneself, to follow a quiet ritual of disengagement from the traffic out there and the traffic in here. When the silence speaks, one has gained companionship with oneself, moved from loneliness to solitude, a necessary prerequisite to individuation.

Connecting with the Lost Child

The influences of early childhood on the first adulthood have long been noted by psychologists. But insufficient attention has been paid to early experience as a potential source of healing during the Middle Passage.

It is not that we have a single child within, perhaps hurt, frightened, codependent or withdrawn in compensation, but a whole host of children, a veritable kindergarten, including the class clown, the artist, the rebel, the spontaneous child at one with the world. Virtually all have been neglected or suppressed. Thus therapy is often enhanced by recovering a sense of their presence. Surely this is one way to take Jesus' observation that to enter the Kingdom of Heaven one must become a child again.

Certainly, we also have to deal with our narcissistic child, our jealous child, our enraged child, whose eruptions are often embarrassing and destructive. But we have more likely forgotten the freedom, the wonderful naivete, the joy even, of life lived freshly. One of the most corrosive experiences of midlife is the sense of futility and joylessness that comes with routine. And, frankly, the free child we all carry is seldom welcome at the office, perhaps not even in the marriage.

So most of all, if we are to heal ourselves, we have to ask what our spontaneous, healthy child wants. For some, the encounter with the free child will be easy; for others the work will be difficult, so deeply buried is this denied essence. When Jung experienced the Middle Passage, he sat on the shores of Lake Zürich and built sand castles, played with toy figures, carved and shaped stones, bringing his rich intellect and intuition into contact with neglected regions of the soul.[103] To his neighbors he might have appeared crazy, but Jung knew that when we are stuck we are saved by what is within. If this free child is not approached consciously, he or she will break through unconsciously and often disruptively. It is the difference between becoming childlike, that is, in touch with one's inner child, and being childish.

At midlife, one must finally ask that inner child what it needs, what it wants. Left behind during the ego-construction of the first adulthood is a natural orientation to the world and the many talents, interests and enthusiasms that go with it. We are rewarded for specialization, not only at work but in intimate relationships. The talent left behind heals when brought to the surface and utilized. Given the kaleidoscopic character of the Self, only a few facets will ever be lived. This incompleteness is part of the existential tragedy, but the more that can be lived, the richer one's life will be.

We have already noted how in midlife the flow of feeling is often

---

[103] *Memories, Dreams, Reflections,* pp. 170ff.

blocked by boredom or depression. This is really saying that our own nature is too narrowly channeled and has become dammed up. Where there is play, there is the life force. Why is it so many courtship scenes in films show a couple swinging on park swings or crashing into the surf, acting like kids again? This cliché too has its truth. Motivating the emerging relationship is the need and hope to reconnect with one's free child.

The Middle Passage provides an unparalleled opportunity to ask, "What would my inner child enjoy?" Go back and take music lessons; take that art class, talent be damned; rediscover play. As a friend of mine who interviewed a number of retirees once said, he never once heard the wish that one had spent more time at the office. We can still attend to outer obligations, work and relationship, but we must make time for the lost child.

The Passionate Life

Joseph Campbell, when asked how one should live, was fond of saying, "Follow your bliss."[104] He understood how most of the time we live according to the dictates of parents and culture, losing the best part of ourselves along the way. Some have trouble with the word "bliss," equating it with narcissism or with some unrealistic space-trip. I understand him to be referring to the soul's journey, including all the suffering and sacrifice this involves. Personally, I am more inclined to say, "Follow your passion."

Passion is what fuels us and, like vocation, is less a choice than a summons. When he was entering his tenth decade, sculptor Henry Moore was asked how he could continue so richly and he replied that he had had a passion so great that he could never chip it all away.[105] Similarly, Yeats was writing poetry even on his death bed. In the last year of his life he wrote of himself as "the wild old wicked man."[106] And the Greek novelist Kazantzakis advised, "Leave nothing for death to take, nothing but a few bones."[107] I am citing literary figures not only because they leave a paper trail, but because the artist is near the fire all the time. Anyone who has attempted to be genuinely creative knows what hard work it is, how suffering is unavoidable, and yet how satisfying can be the sense of process and completion.

---

104 See, for instance, *This Business of the Gods,* pp. 104-108.
105 Roger Berthoud, *The Life of Henry Moore,* p. 420.
106 *The Collected Poems of W.B. Yeats,* p. 307.
107 *The Saviors of God,* p. 102.

In the Middle Passage we are invited to find our passion. It is an imperative to find that which draws us so deeply into life and our own nature that it hurts, for that experience transforms us.

We may, as believers in reincarnation have it, return anew and have other chances to work out other possibilities, but even then, that is another life, not this one. We are called to this present life to live it most fully. We cannot approach death and infirmity hesitant and ashamed, whining about the past. If we are here to be fully ourselves, then surely now is the time.

To find and follow one's passion is not necessarily to take off, as Gauguin did to Tahiti, for there are commitments to honor, people whose lives are affected by our decisions, and something to say for staying a course to which we have a moral responsibility. Yet we are still obliged to live our passion lest our lives remain trivial and provisional, as if some day all would become clear and choices easy. Life is seldom clear and easy; yet choice is what defines and validates a life.

Fear of our own depths is the enemy. We do not feel we have permission? At midlife permission is to be seized, not requested. Fear, not others, is the enemy. But if we are afraid of our own depth, our passionate capacities, we ought to be even more afraid of the unlived life.

Here are some important axioms:

1) Life without passion is life without depth.

2) Passion, while dangerous to order, predictability and sometimes sanity, is the expression of the life force.

3) One cannot draw near the gods, the archetypal depths, without risking the largeness of life which they demand and passion provides.

4) Finding and following one's passion serves one's individuation.

When we become conscious of the largeness of our lives and reach beyond the confines of childhood and ethnocentricity, we then must say yes to our journey and risk all. Rilke wrote a poem titled "The Archaic Torso of Apollo," in which the speaker is examining an antique sculpture, every crack and curve in the finely wrought stone. And then he realizes that he is, in turn, being "watched" by the sculpture. The poem ends with the sudden, shocking imperative: "You must change your life!"[108] My understanding of this is that when one has been in the presence of the truly creative, the imaginatively bold, then one cannot feign unconsciousness. One

---

[108] *Selected Poems of Rainer Maria Rilke,* p. 147.

is similarly summoned to largeness of soul, boldness of action. Finding and following our passion, that which touches us so deeply that it both hurts and feels right, serves individuation by pulling our potential from the depths. As with vocation, the ego is not in charge; it can only run away or give assent. "Not my will but Thine." Living passionately renews one when the old life has grown stale. Living passionately is the only way to love life.

The Swamplands of the Soul

The goal of individuation is wholeness, as much as we can accomplish, not the triumph of the ego. A number of years ago I stunned an early morning class by observing that if we live long enough everyone we love will leave us. The corollary is that if we do not live long enough we will have left them.

While the logic is indisputable, the reaction of the class was rather subdued and hinted of protest. Such protest comes not from the cognitive mind, of course, but from the child within who depends on the Other to always be there. Loss of that which we desire is a major overthrow to the ego, just as the overthrow of the assumptions of the first adulthood launches us reluctantly into the Middle Passage. One of the grandest of those illusions is that there is some Ultima Thule called Happiness, a real state which one can discover and in which one can live permanently. Sadly, our lot more often is to wallow in the swamplands of the soul, victimized by sundry dismal denizens.

The denizens in the swamp are loneliness, loss, grief, doubt, depression, despair, anxiety, guilt and betrayal, for starters. But, fortunately, the ego is not the all-powerful commander it presumes to be. The psyche has a purposiveness which lies beyond the powers of conscious control, and our task is to live through these states and find their meaning. Grief, for example, is the occasion for acknowledging the value of that which has been experienced. Because it has been experienced, it cannot be wholly lost. It is retained in the bones and in the memory, to serve and guide the life to come. Or take doubt. Necessity has been called the mother of invention, but doubt is. Doubt may be threatening in its openness, but doubt nonetheless opens. All great advances in human understanding have come out of doubt. Even depression carries a useful message, that something vital has been "pressed down."

Rather than run from the swampland, we are invited to wade in and see what nascent life awaits. Each of these swampland regions represents a current of the psyche whose meaning can be found if we are courageous enough to ride it. When the ship of the Middle Passage is heaving in the swamp we must ask: "What does this mean to me? What is my psyche telling me? What am I to do about it?"

It takes courage to face one's emotional states directly and to dialogue with them. But therein lies the key to personal integrity. In the swamplands of the soul there is meaning and the call to enlarge consciousness. To take this on is the greatest responsibility in life. We alone can grasp the ship's wheel. And when we do, the terror is compensated by meaning, by dignity, by purpose.

The Great Dialectic

Jung employed one of those portmanteau German words, *Auseinandersetzung,* to describe the necessary dialogue with ourselves. One might translate the concept as "setting one thing out over against the other," figuratively depicting a confrontation or dialectic. It is what occurs, for instance, between analyst and analysand and within the unconscious of each.

How is this dialogue to be furthered? Already suggested are the daily questions, "Who am I in this situation, what voice(s) do I hear?" as well as daily meditation and perhaps a more active form of reflection such as keeping a journal.

At the beginning of this book I suggested that our view of the world was not unlike that of looking through the prism of childhood and culture, a lens that refracts the light and distorts our vision. Certain experiences of life become internalized and reinforced, split off, and then assert control over the present when, as complexes, they invade and overwhelm consciousness. We are driven, then, to an obvious question: "Who am I if I am not my ego and not my complexes?" To deal with this dilemma we must embark on the great dialectic. When we move from the ego-world axis, which animates and preoccupies the first part of life, then we are required to undertake the ego-Self dialogue. The Self, as we have seen, manifests its larger purposiveness through many promptings. Whether they be somatic, affective or imaginal, all are expressions of our need to get back on track.

Perhaps the most useful technique whereby we can participate in the inner dialogue is by working on our dreams. We live in a culture which has grown to disdain the inner life and so sees little value in dreams. But the psyche speaks through dream images, images which may be bizarre to the ego but which incarnate the energies and teleology of the Self. When we can discern the meaning of the images we have access to an incredibly rich wisdom, the likes of which we will find in no book or institution. It is our truth; no one else's. If we can follow and understand at least some of our dreams, then we are better able to know what is right for us, what our true nature calls us to. Nowhere else will we find such accurate information about ourselves than in that rich personal mythology presented to us from the nocturnal depths.

Jung also developed a technique called active imagination. This is unlike Freud's method of free association, nor is it a form of meditation. It is a way of activating an image, through painting, working in clay, dancing or whatever, in order to establish a relationship with the emotional charge it carries. This type of *Auseinandersetzung* not only helps consciousness to find meaning in dream images, it also furthers the dialogue between ego and Self.

In the course of my practice I hear about forty dreams a week. Over time one recognizes recurrent motifs. Yet, just when the ego thinks everything is clear, the psyche will spin a curve and confound understanding. Such work is humbling, but there is none richer for one is in direct relationship with the soul, with the mysterious purpose of the cosmos working in and through us all. Of the hundreds of dream illustrations any analytic therapist could provide, I offer here a couple, admittedly more narrative and coherent than many.

The first dream was from a forty-two-year-old woman who had returned to college after raising her children. She was understandably insecure after having been out of the classroom for many years. Very early in her course work she developed a powerful crush on Professor X. After several months of being in love she dreamt:

> I am walking down the corridor and see Professor Y in her office. She beckons me in. Strangely, she has a penis and we make love on her office floor with the door still open. I am shocked but feel it is right. Afterward, I go back down the corridor and see Professor X coming toward me. I smile knowingly, which puzzles him, and walk on past.

The woman was embarrassed by the dream and hesitated to bring it to therapy, for she feared its frankness and its hint of same-sex love. In fact, it was a very positive dream, showing that a corner had been turned. The crush on Professor X had represented all that up to that point was undeveloped in her own life—her animus, her need for a career and new perspectives. Professor Y, whom she only knew from afar, was for the dreamer a model of a woman who had developed her animus but had also very much retained her femininity. Thus, on the subjective level, making love with Professor Y was really about connection, about integrating the masculine and feminine principles in herself. The connection having occurred in her unconscious through the coital event, she could then know something special about herself which rendered the projection onto Professor X unnecessary. Working with the dream symbolically, and discussing what it would feel like to have that balance of opposites within her, gave the dreamer a better idea of her personal developmental task.

A thirty-six-year-old man dreamt that he had arrived in a beautiful mansion where Shakespeare's *A Mid-Summer Night's Dream* was being performed as a kind of erotic ballet. He was asked to participate in the dance and did so until he received a telephone call from his mother insisting that he return to rescue her from some difficulty. At dream's end he was furious at the interruption of what he had wanted to do, but felt compelled to accede to his mother's demand.

In reality the dreamer had put the width of a continent between himself and his mother, but psychologically he still lived with her. He suffered recurrent depression, swamped as he was by a negative anima, and feared commitment in relationships. The Self had presented the dream to him as a gift, a map which delineated his inner terrain. As far as he had traveled geographically, he was still "checking in" with his parent, still victimized by an oppressed childhood. Meanwhile he was missing out on the "dance of life," which was his association to the Shakespearean ballet. The power of the images confirmed the extent of his wounding and its consequences. In brief, the dream underlined his need to free himself from the mother complex and liberate his anima, which Jung defined as "the archetype of life itself."[109]

The more one sees such diurnal dramas the more one comes to believe in that mysterious power within that Jung called the Self. We are not, in this vast universe, bereft of help, empty of meaning. We have a rich and resonant unconscious which speaks to us through the symptomatology of everyday life as well as through the spindrift of dreams and active imagina-

---

[109] "Archetypes of the Collective Unconscious," *The Archetypes and the Collective Unconscious,* CW 9i, par. 66.

tion. Our task in the Middle Passage is to cooperate, to ask of dream images, "Where in me do they come from, what are my associations and what do they say about my conduct?"

The only way to truly revise one's sense of self is by having this kind of dialogue between ego and Self. One does not have to be in formal therapy, one only needs the courage and the daily discipline to "listen in." When we are able to contain and integrate what we learn, we will not feel lonely in our aloneness. When we can internalize our dialogue while maintaining our contacts with the outer world, we then experience that linkage with the world of the soul previously provided by the ancient myths and religions. We learn anew what our ancestors knew, that the darkness is luminous, that the silence speaks. When we have the courage and discipline to go within, to experience the great dialectic with the soul, then we regain a foothold in the eternal.

Momento Mori

Jeremy Bentham, the nineteenth-century English social philosopher and economist, was by all standards a brilliant man. Until a few years ago, if one were among the elect, one could meet him, so to speak, at the London School of Economics. Mr. Bentham, it seems, left a stipend in his will for an annual dinner on his behalf. All well and good. The stipulation was that His Embalmed Sameness was to be wheeled out and placed at the head of the table. One wonders what the smart conversation at such a dinner might be. Would it be gauche to observe that the host is looking rather wan?

The story of Jeremy Bentham is reflective of Western culture. With the erosion of mythic underpinnings, with the transference of self-worth onto material acquisition and social status, modern culture has rendered death the enemy. It is said that mortality is now the only inappropriate topic for a cocktail party. As social commentators like Jessica Mitford *(The American Way of Death)*, Ernest Becker *(The Denial of Death)* and Elizabeth Kubler-Ross *(On Death and Dying)* have observed, America in particular has a problem with the central fact of life, that we are all dying.

This obvious fact is fraught with implications. During the Middle Passage both the magical thinking of childhood and the heroic thinking of the first adulthood are replaced by the grim awareness of time and finitude. The same force, eros, which brings us life, also consumes us. As Dylan Thomas expressed it so succinctly, "The force that through the green fuse drives the flower is my destroyer."[110] The green eros of youth, like the fuse which consumes itself, is confronted at midlife with the stunned sense of its mortality. No wonder, then, the older men who run off with "sweet young things," the women who have collagen treatments, the tucks and nips to hide the advance of time, the sweating and grunting in health spas. Fear of aging and death animates these behaviors.

Why do we wish to remain young? It might be nice to trade in some body parts for more flexible ones, but why would one wish to step back into a sophomoric past? The answer is immediately clear, that one does not wish to take on life as a development rather than a fixation, that one is not prepared to see it as a series of deaths and rebirths, that one is really not up to the fullness of the journey and would prefer to tarry awhile in the known and comfortable. So plastic surgery erases the epaulets of life's campaigns, and adolescence rules the culture.

The Greek myth of Tithonus is about a man who was immortal but continued to age physically. As his body withered he pleaded with the gods for mortality, which they granted. It is the story of Jeremy Bentham and all of us. Time pulls us back down to dust.

It is perfectly natural at midlife to feel distress about the diminution of energy and the undoing of all we have labored to secure. But underneath this distress there is an invitation. The invitation is to shift gears for the next part of the journey, to move from outer acquisition to inner development. Seen from the perspective of the first adulthood, the second half of life is a slow horror show. We lose friends, mates, children, social status, and then our lives. Yet, if it is true, as all religions attest, that the gods intend what nature knows, then we must accede to the greater wisdom of the process. Rather than operate from the perspective of youth, which can only imagine security in terms of ego, surely the greater achievement is to acquire enough tensile strength to affirm the larger rhythm of our whole lifespan.

I have had the privilege to attend some who were dying more consciously than most. One of them, Angela, sat in the same room in which I now sit and said, "I wish it wasn't happening to me this way, but this is the best thing that ever happened to me." She was acknowledging that the cancer consuming her had, finally, summoned her to life. She had led a

---

[110] "The Force That Through the Green Fuse Drives the Flower," *Collected Poems,* p. 10.

good, responsible, honorable life, but she had never known herself. During her analysis she activated untouched parts of herself; she learned music, karate and painting. I was awed by her courage and growing humanity, her simple wisdom. By the time she died she had won through to something larger than herself: the wonderful humility and grandeur of her journey. This person who came to me for help has helped me many times since.

The suffering of the Middle Passage can be transformed into such gains. Ironically, what is gained is a perspective on loss, for relinquishing old ego certainties opens one to a much larger reality. If we were immortal, nothing would really matter, nothing would really count. But we are not immortal, so each choice matters. It is through making choices that we become human and find our personal sense of meaning. The paradox, then, is that the worth and dignity, the terror and promise, of human existence, depend on mortality. This is what Wallace Stevens meant by the observation that "Death is the mother of beauty."[111] The beauty comes out of terror, and so does the desire to affirm—so much terror, so much beauty.

We know we have survived the Middle Passage when we no longer cling to who we were, no longer seek fame or fortune or the appearance of youth. The sense of life as a slow taking away, the inexorable experience of irreplaceable loss, is transformed by relinquishing the old ego attachments and affirming one's deepening descent into the mystery.

As always, the poet has captured this paradox, noted two millennia ago by Jesus, that to win life we must learn to lose it. In his ninth "Duino Elegy," Rilke says of our mortal cycle,

> You were always right and your sacred
> revelation is the intimate death.
> Behold, I'm alive. On what?
> Neither childhood nor future
> grows less . . . surplus of existence
> is welling up in my heart.[112]

The paradox is that only through relinquishing all that we have sought do we transcend the delusory guarantee of security and identity; all sought let go. Then, most strangely, surplus of existence floods our heart. Then we move from the knowledge of the head, important as it sometimes is, to the wisdom of the heart.

---

[111] "Sunday Morning," *The Collected Poems of Wallace Stevens,* p. 106.
[112] *Duino Elegies,* p. 73.

This Luminous Pause

I know no better definition of life than Jung's, that "life is a luminous pause between two great mysteries which yet are one."[113] The mystery which can be known by the narrow band of being we call consciousness is not the whole mystery. We never arrive at the day when we know finally and for sure what the journey has been about. We are only called to live it as consciously as we can.

The modern Greek poet Cavafy has caught the paradox, that perhaps the goal of the journey is the journey itself. His poem is titled "Ithaca," which city was both the place of departure and the goal of Odysseus, prototype of the wanderer in us all. After admonishing Odysseus to pray that his road be long, the adventures many, the poet urges him not to rush his return. And, if he should at last pull into the harbor of his homeland, to remember that

> Ithaca has given you the beautiful voyage.
> Without her you would never have taken the road.
> But she has nothing more to give you.
> And if you find her poor, Ithaca has not defrauded you.
> With the great wisdom you have gained, with so much experience
> you must surely have understood by then what Ithacas mean.[114]

Our Ithacas are not places of arrival or places of rest, but energies which activate and fuel our journey.

During the second half of life, whenever it may come, the old ego world may still require fidelity. But one's sense of reality is far less dependent upon it. Yes, the loss of collective roles is a kind of death, but the conscious letting go may also begin a process of transformation which we are wise to assist rather than impede. After we turn this spiritual corner, a lot of the old ego-urgencies no longer seem important.

A sign that a person has not made the Middle Passage is that he or she is still caught in ego-building activities of the first adulthood. One has not yet learned that they only represent projections onto finite and fallible icons. They are illusory idols which, though necessary early in life, may later cause us to lose sight of the journey. The journey itself, of course, is symbolic, an image for movement, for development, for eros over thanatos, the effort to incarnate meaning. Our task at midlife is to be

---

113 *Letters,* vol. 1, p. 483.
114 *The Complete Poems of Cavafy,* pp. 36-37.

strong enough to relinquish the ego-urgencies of the first half and open ourselves to a greater wonder.

The experience of crisis at midlife is the collapse not of our essential selves, but of our assumptions. As we look around to those who have gone before, we naturally look for models, paradigms of behavior and attitude. The assumption is that if we follow their program we will eventually feel affirmed in who we are and will learn what life means. When that turns out not to be true, we feel disillusioned, anxious, even betrayed. We learn that no one really knows what life means or what the mysteries are. Those who say they do are either still caught in their projections or are hucksters; at best, they are testifying to their own truth, not ours. No gurus, then, for each person's path is different.

Jung reminds us that the pain we feel is the soul-suffering of those who have tried to "content themselves with inadequate or wrong answers to the questions of life."[115] So, if we recognize that our lives are constricted, our horizons limited, our prisms primitive, then we either jump ship or embrace the journey. For those who worry about the impact of their journey on others, we need to remember that our best way of helping them is by living our own life so clearly that they are free to live theirs. Jung felt this was especially true with regard to parents and children. Rilke writes:

> Sometimes a man stands up during supper
> and walks outdoors, and keeps on walking,
> because of a church that stands somewhere in the East.
> And his children say blessings on him as if he were dead.
> And another man, who remains inside his own house,
> stays there, inside the dishes and in the glasses,
> so that his children have to go far out into the world
> toward that same church, which he forgot.[116]

After the Middle Passage, no one can say where the journey will take us. We only know that we must accept responsibility for ourselves, that the path taken by others is not necessarily for us, and that what we are ultimately seeking lies within, not out there. As the Grail legend suggested centuries ago, it is "a shameful thing to take the path others have trod."[117] It is only from within that we perceive the promptings of the

---

[115] See above, note 90.

[116] *Selected Poems of Rainer Maria Rilke*, p. 49.

[117] Chretien de Troyes, *The Story of the Grail*, p. 94.

soul, and it is this emphasis on inner rather than outer truth that distinguishes the second adulthood from the first. Again, Jung reminds us: "Only the man who can consciously assent to the power of the inner voice becomes a personality."[118]

The act of consciousness is central; otherwise we are overrun by the complexes. The hero in each of us is required to answer the call of individuation. We must turn away from the cacaphony of the outer world to hear the inner voice. When we can dare to live its promptings, then we achieve personhood. We may become strangers to those who thought they knew us, but at least we are no longer strangers to ourselves.

The conscious experience of the Middle Passage requires separating who we are from the sum of the experiences we have internalized. Our thinking then moves from magical to heroic to human. Our relations with others become less dependent, asking less of them and more of ourselves. Our ego takes a beating and we have to reposition ourselves with regard to the outer world—career, relationships, sources of empowerment and satisfaction. In asking more of ourselves, we forego disappointment in others for not delivering what they could never deliver; we acknowledge that their primary responsiblity, just like ours, is their own journey. We become increasingly aware of the finitude of the body and the fragility of all things human.

If our courage holds, the Middle Passage brings us back to life after we have been cut off from it. Strangely, for all the anxiety, there is an awesome sense of freedom as well. We may even come to realize that it does not matter what happens outside as long as we have a vital connection with ourselves. The new-found relationship with the inner life more than balances losses in the outer. The richness of the soul's journey proves at least as rewarding as worldly achievement.

Recall Jung's central question. "Are we related to something infinite or not?"[119] We either embody some essential or our life is wasted. A great mysterious energy is embodied at conception, bides awhile and finally goes elsewhere. Let us be gracious hosts, let us consciously assent to the luminous pause.

In the end, let us earn Rilke's words as our epitaph:

---

[118] "The Development of Personality," *The Development of Personality,* CW 17, par. 308.

[119] See above, note 98.

I live my life in growing orbits
which move out over the things of the world.
Perhaps I can never achieve the last,
but that will be my attempt.
I am circling around God, around the ancient tower,
and I have been circling for a thousand years,
and I still don't know if I am a falcon, or a storm,
or a great song.[120]

---

[120] *Selected Poems of Rainer Maria Rilke,* p. 13.

Select Bibliography

On Midlife

Sharp, Daryl. *The Survival Papers: Anatomy of a Midlife Crisis.* Toronto: Inner City Books, 1988.

Sheehy, Gail. *Passages: Predictable Crises of Adult Life.* New York: Bantam, 1977.

Stein, Murray. *In Mid-Life: A Jungian Perspective.* Dallas: Spring Publications, Inc., 1983.

On Women

Carlson, Kathie. *In Her Image: The Unhealed Daughter's Search for Her Mother.* Boston: Shambhala Publications, Inc., 1988.

Godwin, Gail. *Father Melancholy's Daughter.* New York: Morrow, 1991.

Johnson, Robert. *She: Understanding Feminine Psychology.* New York: Harper and Row, 1977.

Leonard, Linda. *The Wounded Woman: Healing the Father-Daughter Relationship.* Boston: Shambhala Publications, Inc., 1983.

McNeely, Deldon Anne. *Animus Aeternus: Exploring the Inner Masculine.* Toronto: Inner City Books, 1991.

Perera, Sylvia Brinton. *Descent to the Goddess: A Way of Initiation for Women.* Toronto: Inner City Books, 1981.

Woodman, Marion. *Addiction to Perfection: The Still Unravished Bride.* Toronto: Inner City Books, 1982.

_____. *The Pregnant Virgin: A Process of Psychological Transformation.* Toronto: Inner City Books, 1985.

_____. *The Ravaged Bridegroom: Masculinity in Women.* Toronto: Inner City Books, 1990.

On Men

Bly, Robert. *Iron John: A Book About Men.* Reading, Mass: Addison-Wesley Publishing Co., 1990.

Corneau, Guy. *Absent Fathers, Lost Sons: The Search for Masculine Identity.* Boston: Shambhala Publications, Inc., 1991.

Hopcke, Robert. *Men's Dreams, Men's Healing.* Boston: Shambhala Publications, Inc.. 1989.

Johnson, Robert. *He: Understanding Male Psychology.* New York: Harper and Row, 1977.

Keen, Sam. *Fire in the Belly: On Being a Man.* New York: Bantam, 1991.

Levinson, Daniel J. *The Seasons of a Man's Life.* New York: Ballantine, 1978.

Monick, Eugene. *Castration and Male Rage: The Phallic Wound.* Toronto: Inner City Books, 1991.

_____. *Phallos: Sacred Image of the Masculine.* Toronto: Inner City Books, 1987.

Moore, Robert and Gillette, Douglas. *King, Warrior, Magician, Lover: Rediscovering the Archetypes of the Mature Masculine.* San Francisco: Harper and Row, 1990.

On Relationship

Bertine, Eleanor. *Close Relationships: Family, Friendship, Marriage.* Toronto: Inner City Books, 1992.

Sanford, John. *The Invisible Partners: How the Male and Female in Each of Us Affects Our Relationships.* New York: Paulist Press, 1980.

Sharp, Daryl. *Getting to Know You: The Inside Out of Relationship.* Toronto: Inner City Books, 1992.

Typology

Kiersey, David and Bates, Marilyn. *Please Understand Me: Character and Temperament Types.* Del Mar, CA: Prometheus Nemesis Press, 1984.

Sharp, Daryl. *Personality Types: Jung's Model of Typology.* Toronto: Inner City Books, 1987.

Inner Work

Abrams, Jeremiah. *Reclaiming the Inner Child.* Los Angeles: Jeremy P. Tarcher, Inc., 1990.

Carotenuto, Aldo. *Eros and Pathos: Shades of Love and Suffering.* Toronto: Inner City Books, 1989

Hall, James. *Jungian Dream Interpretation: A Handbook of Theory and Practice.* Toronto: Inner City Books, 1983.

_____. *The Jungian Experience: Analysis and Individuation.* Toronto: Inner City Books, 1986.

Jaffe, Lawrence W. *Liberating the Heart: Sprituality and Jungian Psychology.* Toronto: Inner City Books, 1990.

Johnson, Robert. *Inner Work: Using Dreams and Active Imagination for Personal Growth.* San Francisco: Harper and Row, 1986.

Storr, Anthony. *On Solitude: A Return to the Self.* New York: Ballantine Books, 1988.

General Bibliography

Agee, James. *A Death in the Family.* New York: Bantam, 1969.

Alighieri, Dante, *The Comedy of Dante Alighieri.* Trans. Dorothy Sayers. New York: Basic Books, 1963.

Apollonaire, Guillaume. In *An Anthology of French Poetry from Nerval to Valery in English Translation.* New York: Doubleday Anchor Books, 1962.

Aristotle. *Poetics.* Ed. and trans. Francis Ferguson. New York: Hill and Wang, 1961.

Arnold, Matthew. *Poetry and Criticism of Matthew Arnold,* New York: Houghton Mifflin, 1961.

Baudelaire, Charles. In *An Anthology of French Poetry from Nerval to Valery in English Translation.* New York: Doubleday Anchor Books, 1962.

Bernbaum, Ernest, ed. *Anthology of Romanticism.* New York: The Ronald Press Co., 1948.

Berthoud, Roger. *The Life of Henry Moore.* New York: Dutton, 1987.

Bonhoefer, Dietrich. *Letters and Papers from Prison.* Trans. Eberhard Bethage. New York: MacMillan, 1953.

Campbell, Joseph. *The Power of Myth.* With Bill Moyers. New York: Doubleday, 1988.

_____. *This Business of the Gods . . .* Based on the documentary film series of the same name. Joseph Campbell in conversation with Fraser Boa. Caledon East, ON: Windrose Films Ltd., 1989.

Cavafy, C.P. *The Complete Poems of Cavafy.* Trans. Rae Dalven. New York: Harcourt, Brace and World, 1961.

Cheever, John. *The Stories of John Cheever.* New York: Alfred A. Knopf, 1978.

Cummings, E.E. *Poems 1923-1954.* New York: Harcourt, Brace and Co., 1954.

de Troyes, Chretien. *The Story of the Grail.* Trans. R.W. Linker. Chapel Hill: University of North Carolina Press, 1952.

Dostoyevsky, Fyodor. *Notes from Underground.* Trans. Andrew McAndrew. New York: Signet, 1961.

Dunn, Stephen. *Landscape at the End of the Century.* New York: W.W. Norton and Co., 1991.

_____. *Not Dancing*. Pittsburgh: Carnegie-Mellon University Press, 1984.

Eliot, T.S. *The Complete Poems and Plays*. Harcourt, Brace and World, 1952.

_____. In *Critical Theory Since Plato*. Ed. Hazard Adams. New York: Harcourt, Brace, Jovanovich, Inc., 1970.

Ellman, Richard. *Yeats: The Man and the Masks*. New York: Dutton, 1948.

Flaubert, Gustave. *Madame Bovary*. Trans. Paul de Man. New York: W.W. Norton and Co., 1965.

Fry, Christopher. *A Sleep of Prisoners*. New York: Oxford University Press, 1951.

Gilligan, Carol. *In a Different Voice*. Cambridge: Harvard University Press, 1982.

Goethe, Johann Wolfgang von. *Faust*. Trans. Walter Kaufmann. New York: Anchor Books, 1962.

Halpern, Howard M. *How to Break Your Addiction to a Person*. New York: Bantam, 1983.

Heidegger, Martin. *Being and Time*. Trans. John Macquarrie. New York: Harper and Row, 1962.

Hillman, James. *Healing Fiction*. Barrytown, NY: Station Hill Press, 1983.

Hobbes, Thomas. *Selections*. New York: Charles Scribner's Sons, 1930.

Hölderlin, Friedrich. *An Anthology of German Poetry from Hölderlin to Rilke*. Ed. Angel Flores. New York: Doubleday Anchor Books, 1960.

Hugo, Richard. *Making Certain It Goes On: The Collected Poems of Richard Hugo*. New York: W.W. Norton and Co., 1984.

Ibsen, Henrich. *A Doll's House and Other Plays*. New York: Penguin, 1965.

Jung, C.G. *Letters* (Bollingen Series XCV). 2 vols. Trans. R.F.C. Hull. Ed. G. Adler, A. Jaffé. Princeton: Princeton University Press, 1973.

_____. *The Collected Works* (Bollingen Series XX), 20 vols. Trans. R.F.C. Hull. Ed. H. Read, M. Fordham, G. Adler, Wm. McGuire. Princeton: Princeton University Press, 1953-1979.

_____. *Memories, Dreams, Reflections*. Trans. Richard and Clara Winston. Ed. A. Jaffé. New York: Vintage Books, 1965.

Kafka, Franz. *Selected Short Stories of Franz Kafka*. Trans. Willa and Edwin Muir. New York: The Modern Library, 1952.

Kazantzakis, Nikos. *The Last Temptation of Christ.* New York: Simon and Schuster, 1960.

————. *The Saviors of God.* Trans. Kimon Friar. New York: Simon and Schuster, 1960.

Kean, Sam and Valley-Fox, Anne. *Your Mythic Journey.* Los Angeles: Jeremy P. Tarcher, Inc., 1989.

Lincoln, Abraham. *The Lincoln Treasury.* Chicago: Wilcox and Follet, 1950.

Moore, Katherine. *Victorian Wives.* London: Allison and Busby, 1987.

Moore, Marianne. *The Complete Prose of Marianne Moore.* New York: Viking, 1986.

Nietzsche, Friedrich. *The Portable Nietzsche.* Trans. Walter Kaufmann. New York: Viking, 1972.

O'Neill, Eugene. *Complete Plays.* New York: Viking, 1988.

Pagels, Elaine. *The Gnostic Gospels.* New York: Vintage Books, 1981.

Pascal, Blaise. *Pensées.* New York: Dutton, 1958.

Plath, Sylvia. *The Collected Poems.* New York: Harper and Row, 1981.

Price, Martin. *To the Palace of Wisdom.* New York: Doubleday, 1964.

Rilke, Rainer Maria. *Duino Elegies.* Trans. C.F. MacIntyre. Berkeley: University of California Press, 1963.

————. *Letters of Rainer Maria Rilke.* Trans. Jane Green and M.D. Herter Norton. New York: W.W. Norton and Co., 1972.

————. *Letters to a Young Poet.* Trans. M.D. Herter Norton. New York: W.W. Norton and Co., 1962.

————. *Selected Poems of Rainer Maria Rilke.* Trans. Robert Bly. New York: Harper and Row, 1981.

Roethke, Theodore. *The Collected Poems of Theodore Roethke.* New York: Doubleday and Co., 1966.

Roth, Philip. *Goodbye, Columbus and Five Short Stories.* Boston: Houghton Mifflin, 1959.

Stevens, Wallace. *The Collected Poems of Wallace Stevens.* New York: Alfred A. Knopf, 1954.

Terence. *Comedies.* Chicago: Aldine Publishing Co., 1962.

Thomas, Dylan. *Collectred Poems.* New York: New Directions Publishing Co., 1946.

Thoreau, Henry. *The Best of Walden and Civil Disobedience.* New York: Scholastic Books, 1969.

Untermeyer, Louis, ed. *A Concise Treasury of Great Poems.* New York: Simon and Schuster, 1942.

von Franz, Marie-Louise. *Projection and Re-Collection in Jungian Psychology: Reflections of the Soul.* LaSalle, IL: Open Court, 1988.

Wagoner, David. *A Place To Stand.* Bloomington, IN: Indiana University Press, 1958.

Wakoski, Diane. *Emerald Ice: Selected Poems 1962-87.* Santa Rosa, CA: Black Sparrow Press, 1988.

Whitehead, Alfred North. *Nature and Life.* New York: Greenwood Press, 1968.

Wordsworth, William. *Poetical Works of Wordsworth.* New York: Oxford University Press, 1960.

Yeats, William Butler. *The Collected Poems of W.B. Yeats.* New York, MacMillan, 1963.

Permissions

Index

Studies in Jungian Psychology
by Jungian Analysts

Quality Paperbacks

Prices and payment in $US (except in Canada, $Cdn)

Creating a Life: Finding Your Individual Path
James Hollis (Houston) ISBN 0-919123-93-7. 160 pp. $18

Jung and Yoga: The Psyche-Body Connection
Judith Harris (London, Ontario) ISBN 0-919123-95-3. 160 pp. $18

Jungian Psychology Unplugged: My Life as an Elephant
Daryl Sharp (Toronto) ISBN 0-919123-81-3. 160 pp. $18

Conscious Femininity: Interviews with Marion Woodman
Introduction by Marion Woodman (Toronto) ISBN 0-919123-59-7. 160 pp. $18

The Middle Passage: From Misery to Meaning in Midlife
James Hollis (Houston) ISBN 0-919123-60-0. 128 pp. $16

Eros and Pathos: Shades of Love and Suffering
Aldo Carotenuto (Rome) ISBN 0-919123-39-2. 144 pp. $18

Descent to the Goddess: A Way of Initiation for Women
Sylvia Brinton Perera (New York) ISBN 0-919123-05-8. 112 pp. $16

Addiction to Perfection: The Still Unravished Bride
Marion Woodman (Toronto) ISBN 0-919123-11-2. Illustrated. 208 pp. $20pb/$25hc

The Illness That We Are: A Jungian Critique of Christianity
John P. Dourley (Ottawa) ISBN 0-919123-16-3. 128 pp. $16

Coming To Age: The Croning Years and Late-Life Transformation
Jane R. Prétat (Providence) ISBN 0-919123-63-5. 144 pp. $18

Jungian Dream Interpretation: A Handbook of Theory and Practice
James A. Hall, M.D. (Dallas) ISBN 0-919123-12-0. 128 pp. $16

Phallos: Sacred Image of the Masculine
Eugene Monick (Scranton) ISBN 0-919123-26-0. 30 illustrations. 144 pp. $18

The Sacred Prostitute: Eternal Aspect of the Feminine
Nancy Qualls-Corbett (Birmingham) ISBN 0-919123-31-7. 20 illustrations. 176 pp. $20

Personality Types: Jung's Model of Typology
Daryl Sharp (Toronto) ISBN 0-919123-30-9. 128 pp. $16

The Eden Project: In Search of the Magical Other
James Hollis (Houston) ISBN 0-919123-80-5. 160 pp. $18

Discounts: any 3-5 books, 10%; 6-9 books, 20%; 10 or more, 25%
Add Postage/Handling: 1-2 books, $3 surface ($6 air); 3-4 books, $5 surface ($10 air);
5-9 books, $10 surface ($15 air); 10 or more, free surface ($20 air)

Ask for **Jung at Heart** newsletter and free Catalogue of **over 100 titles**

INNER CITY BOOKS
Box 1271, Station Q, Toronto, ON M4T 2P4, Canada

Tel. (416) 927-0355 / Fax (416) 924-1814 / E-mail: sales@innercitybooks.net